SPIRITS DISTILLED

Thanks for their most welcome advice to fellow Taste and Flavour pioneers: Tony Hart, Dave Broom, Tomas Estes, Nicholas Faith, Ian Wisniewski and Desmond Payne. Special thanks to Michael Butt for his wisdom on cocktails.

SPIRITS DISTILLED

Mark Ridgwell

with cocktails mixed by Michael Butt

First published in Great Britain in 2012
This revised edition published in 2016 by
Infinite Ideas Limited
36 St Giles
Oxford, OX1 3LD
United Kingdom
www.infideas.com

A CIP catalogue record for this book is available from the British Library
ISBN 978–1–908984–78–4

Front cover image, courtesy of the London Distillery Company, shows Christina,
one of the Company's stills. The London Distillery Company was founded in
2011 to provide the British public with Genuine British Spirits of the best quality
and without any adulteration.
Photographs on pages 16, 139, 143 and 147 courtesy of BNIC
Photographs on pages 151, 154, 155 and 156 courtesy of BNIA
Diagram on page 14 courtesy of Bacardi Martini
Photographs on pages 60, 61, 62 and 68 courtesy of Phil Bayley
Illustration on page 84 courtesy of the Hampshire Flag Company
Author photograph courtesy of Gino Meenen

Printed in U.S.A.

CONTENTS

1

THE PRINCIPLES OF DISTILLATION

HISTORICAL BACKGROUND

Surprisingly little is known of alcohol's early history, but considerable evidence does confirm that knowledge of fermentation existed in many parts of the world before Christ. As long ago as 3500BC the Chinese distilled extracts from flowers, not for drinking but for use as perfumes, antiseptics, anaesthetics, preservatives and in religious ceremonies. As the Chinese established trade routes across land and sea their knowledge and skills transferred to countries like India, Persia and Egypt, and archaeological finds indicate the use of distillation in South-East Asia by 2500BC. Alexander the Great brought the knowledge back from his conquests of the Persian Empire and Aristotle demonstrated his rudimentary understanding of distillation in a paper he wrote in 350BC. Evidence of early Christian knowledge about distillation was apparent in one sect which likened the soul to volatile elements in distilled wine, believing that when people died, their souls rose to heaven as vapours, there to be reconstituted in a purer form.

The Romans, and then the Christian church, destroyed much of what was thought to be pagan knowledge, but luckily Christianity never took hold in the Arab lands where experimentation with the process of making potable alcohol continued. No certain time or place exists for the arrival of distillation in Western Europe but in an area that is now Iraq, in the eighth century, an Arabic scientist, Geber wrote of distilling wines and condensing the spirit in a 'serpent' or coiled tube immersed in water. Geber's work was translated into Latin in the twelfth century by monks in Salerno, but for the previous five centuries, since 711AD, Arabs had occupied the Iberian Peninsula (Spain) where they codified and perfected the practice of distillation. *Ambix*, the Greek word for a vase with a small opening that was part of the distillation equipment was adopted by the Arabs and changed to *ambiq*, with the equipment being called *alambiq* giving us the word 'alembic' for a still. The Arab word *alkohl*, a fine powder used as an eye cosmetic, gradually came to mean any refined, and so distilled, product, giving rise to the term 'alcohol'.

A chemical physician of the thirteenth century, Arnaud de Villeneuve is credited with being the first European to write and speak openly of an intoxicating spirit obtained through the distillation of wine, and by the end of that century the distillation process was understood and practised across Europe in the monasteries. Distillates continued to be valued more as medicines than enjoyed as drinks but were already known to be useful preservatives and were thought to possess valuable nutrients. These factors, combined with their perceived magical properties, possibly contributed to early recognition of spirits first as the waters of immortality and then as *aqua vitae* or water of life, translated into Gaelic, as *uisge beatha*, into English as 'whisky' and into French, as *eau-de-vie*. Raymond Lully of Majorca, who reputedly learned from Arnaud himself, later described the spirit as an emanation of the divinity, an element newly revealed to man but hidden in antiquity because the human race was then too young to need this beverage, destined to revive the energies of modern decrepitude.

In the fourteenth century armagnac was developed in France. By the fifteenth century, knowledge was moving beyond the monasteries and new spirits were beginning to appear across Europe, including grain-based spirits in Holland, Poland, Russia, Ukraine and Scotland. During the sixteenth and seventeenth centuries distillation skills improved around the world, particularly in Holland. Not only were the Dutch the world's great trading nation at that time, sailing the world and bringing many new products from the tropics back to Europe, but they were probably the most experienced distillers of their day too. At home they distilled exotic spices, nuts and fruits into what would develop into the liqueurs we know so well today; in Spain and France they transformed wines into *brandewijn* or burnt wine which the Europeans shipped to their colonies, fearful of foreign water and seeking protection and comfort in familiar drinks.

The cost of such shipments was high and so, following the earlier success of the Genoese and Venetian merchants shipping exotic spirits like arrack to Europe, the Spanish, Dutch and English explorers were keen to discover similar rewards in their colonies. In South America and the Caribbean the Europeans applied their distillation skills to sugar cane, agave and to the grapes they planted, and created cachaça, rum, mezcal, tequila and pisco. In North America, in the eighteenth century, first rum and then Irish whiskey took root and, in the nineteenth century, scotch began to establish its global reputation at the expense of Irish whiskey. Back in Europe, in the late eighteenth century, the English had discovered genever on the battlefields of Holland only to suffer a century later from excess domestic consumption of the gin they went on to create as their first commercially produced spirit.

The earliest evidence of alcoholic drinks in China is wine jars dated to 7000BC and, as early as the eleventh century BC, a Chinese Imperial edict states that the use of alcohol in moderation is prescribed by heaven. By Marco Polo's time, 1234–1324, alcohol was drunk daily and provided a major source of income to the treasury but it was not until the nineteenth century that distilled drinks became really popular in China. *Baijiu*, often translated as 'wine' or 'white wine', is the name for the Chinese distilled alcohol of between 40% and 60% ABV.

Soju, a name derived from the Chinese and meaning 'burned liquor', is today's largest spirit category. The spirit is native to Korea and was first distilled during the thirteenth century with skills passed on from the Persians to the Mongol invaders of Korea. The origins of the Japanese spirit 'shochu', a name also derived from the Chinese, are unclear but early descriptions as 'arak', suggest its roots lay in the Middle East. It originated in Kagoshima and records suggest it has been distilled since the sixteenth century at least.

By the eighteenth century, production of spirits was global but most remained raw and even dangerous, obliging distillers to use flavourings to disguise the taste. Governments began to license distilleries, to ensure that only safe, potable spirits were sold and to raise revenues. In the nineteenth century distillation became a more exact science and the benefits of maturation became better understood. Spirit production became commercialized and brands started to offer consistency and quality guarantees.

RAW MATERIALS

Distillation cannot create alcohol. The distillation process can only concentrate alcohols already present in a liquid. Any raw materials, be they fruit, grain, vegetables or plants can be used as a base for distillation so long as they contain sugars able to be converted directly into alcohol by fermentation or starches capable of conversion into sugars.

Historically, spirits were made from what the local environment provided. Grain, vegetables and herbs were usual in the colder climates, fruits and spices in the warmer zones and sugar cane in the tropics. Today, some plants are used to produce spirits that enjoy exclusive designations, specific to one country or to delineated regions within countries.

When sugar is naturally present, as in fruit or molasses, prior preparation is not required, except perhaps heating; yeasts can work on the sugars already present in the raw material and convert them into alcohol. When sugar is not present in the raw material, as with grain and potatoes, fermentation may only take place after the starches have been converted into fermentable sugars. First, the grain or vegetables may be cooked to break down the protein walls that enclose the starch cells. Some distillers may then add commercially produced enzymes to convert the starch into fermentable sugars. Others may add a small amount of malt to achieve the same purpose with natural enzymes.

To produce malt, barley is steeped in warm water to encourage it to grow. (Barley is a good source of amylase, the enzyme that seeds use to convert starch food reserves into sugars.) The protein walls break down, triggering these natural enzymes to convert the starch within the grains into the sugars required to feed the plant's emerging shoots. The wet, warm malt will be allowed to germinate and what is now called 'green malt' will begin to grow shoots and roots. To preserve the enzymes it is vital that this growth is halted. The green malt is dried either in a closed, smoke-free kiln or, when additional flavouring is required, it is spread out on a perforated floor over burning peat. The resulting barley malt may then be stored, ready to be added to a mash of prepared grain or vegetables to assist the conversion of their starches into soluble, fermentable sugars.

Once fermentable sugars are present, yeast, a living microorganism, natural or cultivated, is added to the sugar-rich liquid to convert the sugars into numerous different alcohols, carbon dioxide and heat. Yeast spores are all around us but not all are the same. Some producers will use the natural yeasts that are found on the surface of the raw materials and in the air. Some will cultivate a strain and hand it down from generation to generation to maintain a product's individuality. Others will buy industry yeasts.

Whatever the choice, yeasts can contribute a significant range of aromas and flavours to complement the characteristics already present in the raw materials. These 'congeners' consist of aldehydes, esters, alcohols and fusel oils, all of which will generate tastes and aromas, some good and some bad, which will be concentrated by the process of distillation. Different yeast strains will react with the sugars of different raw materials to produce different combinations of congeners. These, in turn, will create varied tastes and aromas in the finished spirit.

Fermentation is vital to the character and quality of any distilled spirit and, generally speaking, the slower the fermentation the greater the potential for character in a finished spirit.

Some spirits must be made from one raw material. For example, when no fruit is specified on the label, brandy must be made from grapes. Rum must be made from sugar cane and tequila from the blue agave plant. Others, like vodka, can be made from a range of raw materials, including grain, molasses, vegetables and fruit. Some, such as gin, are neutral spirit flavoured with additional ingredients. Others, such as liqueurs, may be flavoured and sweetened. The only universal stipulation today is that potable alcohol must be of agricultural origin.

DISTILLATION

Distillation is the process of isolating and separating alcohols by boiling or freezing an alcoholic wash; the lower the level of alcohol in the initial fermented wash, the greater the potential for distillation to concentrate not only the alcohols but also the flavours they carry. Distillation separates alcohols from water because alcohols and water boil and evaporate at different temperatures. After the alcohol vapours are separated from the water they cool and condense into a liquid containing a higher percentage of alcohol and a greater concentration of the flavour carrying compounds within the alcohols. Alcohols that carry unwanted compounds may be drawn off and redistilled or removed with the solids that remain in the still.

For potable spirits the relevant factor is that ethyl alcohol, also called ethanol, boils at 78.4°C and water at 100°C. By heating the base alcoholic wash, ethanol and other alcohols that vaporize at lower and higher temperatures than water and the congeners they carry can be eliminated as they condense or can be drawn off and collected in concentrated form leaving behind most, but not all, of the water and solids. Each distiller monitors the distillation run and collects the alcohols required for the final spirit, returning some for further distillation and discarding others along with the remaining liquid and solids. The extended process of removing undesirable compounds from the distillate is called rectification.

During the distillation process the more volatile alcohols first vaporize as 'heads' or 'foreshots'. A proportion of these will be too low in alcohol or of poor quality and so will be redistilled. Some, like methanol, are potentially poisonous and so are removed or significantly reduced in quantity, others, called 'esters', may be retained to contribute light, fruity and flowery characteristics to the final spirit.

The middle cut or 'heart' of the distillate, including ethyl alcohol and, if desirable, other potable alcohols, is collected and retained for further distillation, maturation or immediate bottling. The 'tails' or 'feints', being heavier and less volatile, only vaporize during the latter stage of a distillation run. Some traces of these higher alcohols may be retained along with the middle cut because even minute quantities of these can make a significant contribution to the overall flavour of a finished spirit. Their collection ceases as the heaviest, less palatable compounds, called 'fusel oils' appear, though small quantities even of these may be retained to contribute to the flavour profile of the more pungent spirits.

The congeners created during fermentation and concentrated during distillation provide a spirit with much of its personality and individuality. So, where the distiller makes the cuts and the level of rectification is key to the final character of any spirit. The cuts decide which congeners are retained and which are rejected until, with rectification, almost only ethanol remains. The greater the level of congeners retained in the newly made spirit, the more likely that maturation will be required to make the spirit palatable. However, even in a complex, flavoursome spirit like whisk(e)y, these characterful and aromatic congeners may still account for under 1% of the overall liquid volume.

All spirits are colourless when they exit the still.

PROOF AND STRENGTH

The ability to correctly assess the alcoholic strength of a spirit was, and is, essential to the raising of taxes, Initially, the alcohol content of a spirit was tested by dipping a rag in the liquid and attempting to set fire to it – if it was sufficiently alcoholic the rag would burn. Towards the fifteenth century oil was floated on the surface of the spirit to assess its strength. Later the spirit was mixed with gunpowder and a flame applied. If it caught fire, it was strong enough to be 'proved'. If it exploded, it was stronger and so described as 'overproof'.

Today the strength of spirit is assessed with much greater accuracy and according to three systems.

1. The historic British system measured alcohol levels in terms of 'proof spirit'. The old British 100° proof was equal to 57.15% ABV so spirits bottled above that level were described as overproof.

2. In Europe, during the eighteenth and nineteenth centuries, the hydrometer was used to measure alcohol content and to determine excise taxes based on the Archimedes principle of displacement. This system expresses alcohol as a percentage of pure spirit. A bottle with 40% on the label contains 40% pure alcohol by volume, measured at 20°C. The Organisation Internationale de Métrologie Légale, or OIML requires all alcoholic drinks sold in the EU to state their alcohol content in this way and since 1 January 1980 the British have conformed to this system, referred to as the Gay-Lussac System or OIML.

3. The American system is different to that used in Europe. Proof spirit is equivalent to the number 100 and pure alcohol, 200. So halving the proof stated on American labels will give the strength in terms of percentage alcohol, the OIML system.

Why is the usual bottle strength 40%?

In 1893, Dmitri Mendeleev, a Russian chemist and inventor was appointed director of the Bureau of Weights and Measures and was directed to formulate new state standards for the production of vodka. He determined that the ideal alcohol content was 38% ABV. As a result of his work, in 1894, new standards for vodka were introduced into Russian law. All vodka had to be sold at 40% by weight, rather than by volume, because, this was then a more reliable system of measurement. At the time, distilled spirits were taxed according to their alcoholic strength and, to simplify the taxation calculations, his 38% was rounded up to 40%.

Dmitri Mendeleev

Today, most spirits are bottled at somewhere between 40% and 45% ABV, as much for reasons of taste as tax. A minimum of 37.5% ABV has been introduced, usually for white spirits but, on occasion, for dark spirits too. Some national spirits are bottled at lower strengths. When alcoholic strength drops below 40% ABV many of the more volatile esters that add character to the finished spirit can be lost. Above 50% ABV the alcohol can begin to overwhelm some of the other tastes and aromas.

Excepting lower strengths that may be permitted for some local or national spirits, any alcoholic product below 37.5% cannot be called 'spirit' without adding words such as 'diluted'.

THE STILLS

Distillation is the process of concentrating the alcohols already present in a wash. Rectification is the process of removing undesirable components from a distillate. Both these processes can be made to work, to a greater or lesser efficiency, in two different types of still: a pot still or a column still, or a combination of both.

Pot still

The pot still has not changed for centuries. It is shaped like a large kettle and is made of copper, which heats up and cools down faster than any other metal. Copper absorbs foul-smelling sulphur compounds, producing copper sulphate that can then be physically removed from the liquid as an undesirable element. Copper also removes unwanted heavy fusel oils while contributing no character of its own to the taste of a distillate. Often, even stainless steel column stills have copper heads or copper panels.

The low alcohol wash is boiled in the pot still, using either direct or indirect heat. Vapours rise from the boiling liquid, up the neck and flow along the lyne arm, or swan's neck, into a condenser. Depending on the temperature at which each vaporizes, as they rise and come into contact with increasingly cooler surfaces, initially towards the top of the pot and then in the neck, the vapours condense.

If the vapours condense before they exit the pot or the neck, the condensed alcohols will drop back into the boiling liquid and not pass over into the condenser. This process is called reflux. Vapours that do not reflux condense after they flow into the lyne arm or when they reach the condenser where they are cooled by cold water and collected. The height of the neck and angle of the lyne arm determines the level of reflux and the character of the resulting distillate. A lyne arm that slopes upwards away from the still and a long neck both encourage more reflux and deliver a lighter distillate. A shorter neck and a downward sloping arm create less reflux, allowing more of the heavier, less volatile vapours to pass over and flow into the condenser, resulting in a heavier distillate. The speed of heating also influences reflux. Rapid heating reduces the rate of reflux but only with a risk that more of the undesirable compounds will pass into the condensed distillate.

Pots are not ideal for large-scale production because distillation in pots is slow, not very heat-effective and is labour-intensive. Distillation must be done in batches. To achieve acceptable levels of quality potable alcohol, two or, in some cases, three separate batch distillations are required. The low alcohol liquid first enters the larger still, called the 'wash still'. This shapes the broad character of a new-make spirit and generates 'low wines' of around 30%–35% ABV. The second, called the 'low wines' or 'spirits still' increases the strength and refines the spirit by removing undesirable or unwanted compounds but, even after second and third distillations in a pot still, many of the characteristics and by-products of the base material are retained.

Distillers wanting to retain character from their base materials or to refine or add delicate flavours to a neutral spirit use pot stills but it has been estimated that five distillations in a pot would likely only extract 45% of the available alcohol compared with 95% in a continuous still. This is why production of a truly rectified spirit requires a continuous still.

Continuous still

The patent still people strip the spirit of all it ought to possess. As a man stripped of his garments is still a man, although not fit in such a state to enter into society, so the bare silent spirit is still a spirit!

Truths about Whisky, 1878

The still most widely used today is the continuous, patent or Coffey still, invented in 1827 by Robert Stein, a Scot working in Ireland. However, this device is named after an Irish customs officer, Aeneas Coffey, who retired in 1824 and went on to perfect the process and to patent his version of the design in 1831. Interestingly, he found greater support for the invention in Scotland than in Ireland. This still consists of one vertical column, called the analyzer, connected with one or more additional columns, called rectifiers, each divided into compartments by horizontal plates, some perforated and some not. Steam enters the foot of the analyzer, rises and meets the cold wash that has entered into the top of the analyzer column.

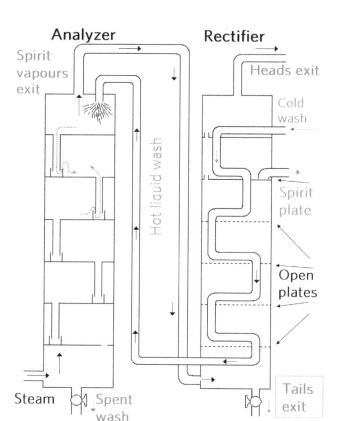

Continuous still

As the wash drops through the plates, it is heated by the hot steam rising in the column. The alcohols in the wash are vaporized as they rise up inside the column, with the steam, to exit out of the top of the analyzer as alcohol-rich vapours. From here the vapours drop down a pipe to enter into the bottom of the rectifier. As these hot vapours rise through the perforated trays in the rectifier they cool and condense at different temperatures, either on 'spirit' plates that are unperforated, to be drawn off and collected by the distiller or on the perforated plates so that they drop down and exit from the foot of the column.

Some distillers may enter their wash into the top of the rectifier, through a pipe that drops down through the rectifier so the hot alcohol-rich vapours heat the wash as it drops. The heated wash then rises up another pipe outside the rectifier, to be sprayed into the top of the analyzer.

The process is continuous, allowing early, volatile alcohols or esters to rise and pass through perforated plates until they condense at the lower temperatures towards the top of the column while the heavier alcohols, feints and fusel oils condense at the higher temperatures towards the foot of the column. The distiller places unperforated spirit plates only where the required vapours condense, allowing these to be drawn off and retained wherever the plates are positioned. Vapours that condense towards the top of the column can yield a very pure and clean spirit of around 85% to 90% ABV but, if condensed lower down, at higher temperatures, a more complex spirit is drawn off at levels of alcohol as low as 50% ABV, containing more impurities and so more character. The nature of distillate that is collected depends on the number of plates used in the still and where they are placed. The addition of extra rectifying columns, each intended to remove specific impurities, concentrates the spirit into a pure and clean distillate in excess of 96% ABV and exceptionally low in impurities.

The continuous still is faster than a pot still and uses less fuel. It produces higher levels of alcohol and in greater quantity than is possible using a pot still. It is used most often, but not always, to yield the higher strength, less complex and more neutral tasting spirits, a requirement particularly welcome in the early nineteenth century when alcohol content by volume was more important than taste. Much of the distillate from column stills then was intended for redistillation into gin or for industrial use.

The spent liquid, still rich in nutrients, flows from the bottom of the column, generally to be dried and sold as animal feed. In America, some of this spent liquid is used in the production of so-called 'sour mash' whiskey (see chapter 12, American whiskey).

Carter Head still

Historically, a Carter Head still incorporated a tall rectifying column, rising from the pot up to the lyne arm but the quality of neutral spirit produced today means this is not always necessary. When gin is produced using a Carter Head still the more delicate botanicals or, if desired, all the botanicals are placed in a basket situated in the lyne arm. This box is perforated so that only the alcoholic vapours that rise from the boiling wash come into contact with the botanicals as they pass through the box into the condenser. This process of vapour distillation avoids any of the botanicals being cooked and extracts the more delicate and subtle flavours and aromatics that might otherwise be destroyed if the botanicals were entered into the wash boiling in the base of the pot. For this reason a Carter Head still may be the choice of gin distillers who want to produce a lighter style of distillate.

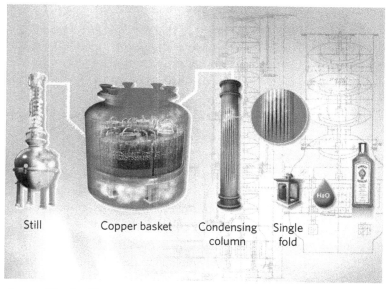

Still   Copper basket   Condensing column   Single fold

Carter Head still

Vacuum still

Vacuum stills allow higher alcohol concentrations to be achieved at lower temperatures meaning they can be more energy efficient and capture more of the available alcohols. They permit the isolation and retention of natural flavours and aromas which might be destroyed or damaged at higher temperatures.

Reflux still

A reflux condenser permits falling pre-condensate to wash the rising vapour, reducing the water and impurity content. The more contact between liquid and vapour, the cleaner and purer the distillate.

Summary of the distillation process

Heating → Conversion → Fermentation → Distillation → Cooling

FINISHING

After distillation there are numerous ways in which the final flavour and character of a spirit may be enhanced.

Ageing

Maturation in wood evolved from the initial convenience of the material. Wood was strong, easy to work and, once made into barrels, easy to move around. Then it was discovered that storage in wood could mellow a harsh and raw spirit, fresh off the still, by allowing the spirit to oxidize and to absorb compounds from the wood.

All oak must be seasoned before use. Kiln drying may be used but this process can cook the tannins and result in some astringency. Natural seasoning of the cut staves in the open air is costly and time consuming but always achieves better results.

Wood toasting and charring

Wood toasting and charring

Wood comprises the cellulose that holds the wood together, sugars that caramelize when wood is toasted, lignin, from the vanillin family of compounds, and tannin. There are over 250 species of oak, belonging to the genus *Quercus*, and oak is the dominant wood used in the production of barrels. Most will use American white oak, Quercus alba, or European oak of which there are two distinct species: Quercus robur, the English oak; and Quercus sessilis, the oak found in most French forests.

Toasting the wood staves used in barrel making enables them to be bent, caramelizes the wood sugars, and helps the transfer of colour. This process also activates the vanillin held in the wood and releases tertiary flavours like coconut and spices.

Charring the wood is a more intense process than toasting and draws more of the sap containing flavours and colour towards the surface, so it lies just below the char. This increases the potential for transfer into the distillate. American oak tends to be charred or heavily burnt while European oak tends to be lightly toasted.

Quercus alba American white oak is grown across North America. Demand has increased in recent years, because bourbon whiskey must always be aged in new wood and because American oak costs less than French oak. It is now the oak most widely used to mature Scotch whisky, rum, tequila and bourbon. Growing tall and straight, Quercus alba is high in vanillin, oak lactones and wood sugars but is relatively low in tannins, which represent scarcely 1% of its mass. Therefore, spirits aged in Quercus alba tend to be lighter in colour and carry sweet notes of vanilla drawn from the vanillin, coconut from the lactones and various spice-like characteristics.

Quercus robur A more porous wood, Quercus robur, is native to most of Europe but France is a significant producer of quality and quantity. It imparts lower levels of vanillin but higher levels of tannin, which can represent almost 10% of its mass. This oak leaches a darker, reddish, mahogany colour along with taste characteristics of cloves and dried fruit.

Maturation in wood performs numerous vital functions. It allows a spirit to breathe through the pores in the wood, in a process called 'oxidation', mellowing the raw spirit and making a significant contribution towards a spirit's final character, quality and texture. The movement of the distillate in and out of the wood causes sugars, flavours, aromas and colours to be absorbed which contributes considerable complexity to the finished spirit. Even if filtration is used later to remove any actual character or colour absorbed from the wood itself, the spirit will still have mellowed during its time in wood. Maturation also promotes esterification, when alcohol oxidizes into aldehydes and then into acids which, in turn, react again with the alcohols themselves.

During maturation more or less is absorbed from the wood, depending on the number of years in the barrel, whether the barrels are charred or toasted, use of new or old wood, first fill or second fill casks and the size of barrel. Hotter climates and higher levels of alcohol both cause more character to be absorbed, more quickly, from the wood. During maturation respective evaporation of water and alcohol varies according to climate. In hot and dry climates evaporation typically varies from 3% to 5% per annum and the other liquids evaporate faster than the alcohol, increasing the overall percentage of alcohol. Where climates are humid and temperatures moderate, evaporation is between 1% and 2% per annum and the alcohol evaporates faster than the other liquids, so lowering the alcohol percentage.

The process of maturation can generate as much as two-thirds of a spirit's final character but the actual level depends on whether the casks have been used previously to age sherry or bourbon. Sherry, barrelled at around 17% ABV is less active and so extracts less from the wood leaving more residues for the spirit to absorb. Bourbon, barrelled at around 62% is more active and extracts a much higher level of the flavour and colour compounds, leaving less for the future spirit to absorb.

Whatever the intention, nothing is guaranteed by age. Wood is a natural product and results can and do vary according to many factors. Age is only one criterion in assessing the complex quality of a spirit.

Blending

The skills of a master blender will ensure consistency and guarantee that the finished spirit conforms to established standards. Blending can also be used to create depth and complexity in a spirit and to enhance its overall character.

Flavouring

Adding flavourings is essential in the production of some spirits. These can be added in four major ways.

1. **Distillation** Flavouring materials are combined with a base spirit, diluted and redistilled in a pot still to extract and attach

the flavours to the alcoholic vapours which then condense into a more concentrated, refined, colourless and flavoured distillate.

2. **Infusion** Flavouring materials are steeped in the base spirit and agitated to yield flavour, aroma and colour. The spirit is separated from the solids and may then be distilled to extract and refine any remaining flavours. If distilled, all colouring will be removed.

3. **Percolation** Spirit is pumped over the flavouring materials to extract the flavours before separation from the solids. The spirit may then be distilled to refine the remaining flavours.

4. **Maceration** Flavouring materials rest in alcohol over time so that the spirit absorbs flavour, aroma and natural colours.

Marrying

Different spirits are combined and left to mature together, often in wood to permit oxidation. Flavours and aromas marry together to create a whole that is intended to be greater than the sum of the parts.

FILTRATION

Some spirits may be polished through filtration while others may be cleaned more thoroughly through the use of activated charcoal. Activated charcoal is wood heated to very high temperatures to produce carbon. The carbon is reheated and activated in the presence of acid and steam to purify and open pores and to produce a very fine, non-toxic black powder. This process increases the carbon's overall surface area and capacity to absorb toxins. Just one gram of activated charcoal has a surface area in excess of 500 square metres.

When bottled and reduced to low temperatures or stored in very cold conditions, certain spirits may become cloudy and throw a deposit. 'Chill filtering' to low temperatures before bottling polishes the finished spirit and converts the compounds that cause this to happen into a deposit that can be extracted by filtration. This process allows the spirit to remain bright and clear at all temperatures. However, removing the deposit also compromises some of the flavour compounds that could otherwise add character and complexity. So, for the sake of clarity, chill filtering can reduce a spirit's overall texture in the mouth and delivery of flavour.

COLOURING

Some producers, wanting their spirits to be clear and bright, may filter out colours absorbed from the wood during maturation. Others, wanting to enrich the colour obtained from the wood or to adjust the colour of a finished spirit to match previous bottlings, may add caramel. Usually additions of caramel and sugar can only be done according to local regulation and such additions may be prohibited in the production of some spirits.

Quiz on distillation principles

1. Which of the following is the correct distillation order?

   A. Heating-conversion-fermentation-distillation
   B. Conversion-heating-fermentation-distillation
   C. Heating-fermentation-conversion-distillation
   D. Conversion-fermentation-heating-distillation

2. What is used to convert fermentable sugars into heat, gas and alcohol?

   A. Starch
   B. Yeast
   C. Caramel
   D. Heat

3. Ethyl alcohol boils at what temperature?

   A. 65.2°C
   B. 74.6°C
   C. 78.4°C
   D. 82.4°C

4. What is the term used to describe the more volatile alcohols that vaporize first during distillation?

   A. Fusel oils
   B. Feints
   C. Aldehydes
   D. Esters

5. The term overproof, when used to describe rums, means rums have been bottled above what level of alcohol?

   A. 40% ABV
   B. 47% ABV
   C. 57% ABV
   D. 65% ABV

6. American proof is equivalent to what percentage level of alcohol?

   A. Equal
   B. Twice
   C. Half
   D. One and a half

7. What is the term used to describe alcohols condensing and falling back into the boiling liquid?

   A. Rectification
   B. Reflux
   C. Returns
   D. Condensing

8. A high level of reflux will contribute to what style of spirit?

   A. More 'spirity'
   B. Heavier
   C. More characterful
   D. Lighter

9. In pot-still distillation the low alcohol wash is entered into what type of still?

A. Wash still
B. Coffey still
C. Spirit still
D. Patent still

10. What type of still is ideal for gin distillers wanting to capture delicate flavours and aromatics?

A. Pot still
B. Reflux still
C. Carter Head still
D. Spirit still

11. What is the purpose of toasting barrel staves?

A. Enables them to be bent
B. Caramelizes the wood sugars
C. Helps to transfer colour
D. All of these

12. Quercus alba is also known as what?

A. European oak
B. American white oak
C. Monlezun oak
D. English oak

13. The process of pumping spirits over flavourings to extract their character is called what?

A Infusion
B. Maceration
C. Percolation
D. Distillation

14. Who were the most experienced distillers in sixteenth and seventeenth century Europe?

   A. Dutch
   B. French
   C. Italian
   D. Spanish

15. Which of these phrases best describes the process of distillation?

   A. The creation of alcohol
   B. The rectification of alcohol
   C. The concentration of alcohol
   D. The measuring of alcohol

16. Which of these raw materials do not require conversion before fermentation?

   A. Corn
   B. Plums
   C. Potatoes
   D. Wheat

17. Storage in wood can do what to a spirit?

   A. Mellow
   B. Add colour
   C. Add complexity
   D. All of these

18. A hot and dry climate will typically do what to a spirit during maturation in wood?

   A. Increase the overall percentage of alcohol
   B. Reduce the annual level of evaporation
   C. Increase the overall percentage of water
   D. Reduce the extracts absorbed from the wood

19. Which of these flavouring processes will result in a colourless distillate?

    A. Maceration
    B. Percolation
    C. Distillation
    D. All of these

20. Which of these production processes mellows a spirit?

    A. Filtration
    B. Oxidation
    C. Percolation
    D. Maceration

2

TASTING SPIRITS

For many, spirits are little more than alcohol and that view is unlikely to change if all we have to aspire to is merely another premium brand or another instantly forgettable cocktail. Attitudes will only change when spirits, like wines, engage our emotions and excite our palates with memorable drinking experiences. For that to happen we need to equip ourselves to make informed choices, not based on brand-speak but on a true understanding of tastes and flavours.

So how do we do that? First, we remember that tasting spirits is different to tasting wines. In spirits the level of alcohol is much higher. To assess and accommodate the potential impact of this alcohol, spirits must be approached with more care, initially from the lip of a glass, held steady in the hand and not twirled as is usual with wines. Otherwise the release of alcohol may temporarily anaesthetize the sensory organs in our nose, bite our tongue and burn our throat rather than serve to increase the mouth feel, provide a lovely warm feeling in the throat or to increase the overall depth and complexity of our experience.

Alcohol in spirits, or the lack of it, is key to defining our taste experience. It may enhance and accentuate the flavours in cocktails and long drinks. It may help to enrich texture and to extend the finish. Equally, an unbalanced level or lack of alcohol may well diminish all of these experiences.

What is certain is that a spirit's level of alcohol by volume is high compared with wines but the quantity of alcohol actually consumed when drinking a spirit by the glass compared with a wine is usually significantly less. For example: a 175 ml glass of wine at 14% ABV holds 24.5 ml of alcohol whereas a 35 ml measure of spirits at 40% ABV holds 14 ml of alcohol.

Tasting is a very personal and subjective exercise. Sometimes our descriptions may help others to find the words they are looking for to describe their own experiences, but they are just as likely to confuse. So, the key to tasting spirits must be to record and share our experiences in a basic language and according to a recognizable structure. Only then can any more personal and creative thoughts add useful weight to our description of the experience.

When tasting spirits it is also wise not to look for winners or losers but to search instead for differences and to apply our knowledge of how the different spirits are made to understanding why each tastes the way it does. It may also be helpful to memorize key characteristics that broadly describe the individuality of each spirit category along with those that help to differentiate between spirits within each category.

What must never be forgotten is that the word 'tasting' is a misnomer. The true challenge in tasting spirits must be to use all our sensory organs to evaluate an experience. On our palate we can taste only five things: salt, sour, sweet, bitter, and a tongue-coating, long-lasting, savoury taste that a Japanese term, umami, is now used to describe. Flavour, however, is a perception that interprets information received from all five of our senses. Flavour is the cognitive, post-sensory perception that forms in our brains. In summary:

- Taste is made up of five pieces of information.

- Flavour is infinite.

- Taste is chemical.

- Flavour is an entirely personal experience created in our mind which we use words to communicate to others.

Our eyes see only three primary colours, but we are careful not to communicate too broad a description of what we see. Many so-called white spirits have hints of colour. Brown spirits are many shades of brown, from beige to mahogany. Also, our eyes can detect more than just colour. Indeed, the colour itself should be our last observation.

First assess the grip a spirit has to the glass; the greater the grip of the 'legs' that drop down the glass and the slower they fall, the greater the potential level of alcohol and/or quantity of congeners (flavour compounds). Before describing the colour itself, assess the clarity of the sample and then the intensity of the colour. Remember, we rarely describe a setting sun as red or a sky as blue. More likely, we say something like deep red or light blue. With spirits too, some are pale in colour while others are deep and intense.

Next we should recognize that our nose is our most useful sensory organ. Compared with those three primary colours and five tastes, there are thirty-two primary aromas. Our nose has five to ten million receptors capable of detecting aromas whereas our tongue has only nine thousand taste buds; thus, our nose is estimated to be ten thousand times more sensitive than our palate.

When we say that something tastes nice it is probable that 80% of the experience is detected in our nose. Certainly the nose provides excellent opportunities to test the initial judgements we make, based on colour. For example the nose can assess whether the colour is more likely generated by the addition of caramel or by maturation in wood.

As with our eyes, we must try to be precise with our observations on aroma. For example: freshness could be youthful, refreshing, raw or unbalanced. Again, we should leave specific descriptions of the actual aromas until last. First it is better to note whether the nose is open or closed, neutral or pungent, spirity or balanced, simple or complex. Only then should we assess the specific aromas, be they floral or phenolic, fruity or spicy, or any of the other aromatic qualities that can be found in spirits across and within the individual categories.

For the tasting itself, we should use the whole of our palate, looking for sweetness on the tip of the tongue, bitterness towards the back and salty and sour characteristics to the sides before assessing whether length and finish extends the experience or disappoints. As with the eyes and nose, any specific characteristics should be left until last. Assess sweetness, alcohol, woodiness, texture, balance and intensity. Only then, as with the aromas, record the specific taste characteristics.

Sometimes experiences will develop as expected and sometimes not; sometimes, primary sweetness can become dry; sometimes a rich, full colour can contrast with a featureless, thin nose and a disappointing texture on the palate. Only by using all our senses to appreciate the overall character of a spirit can we make fair and useful judgements on overall quality. Employing a descriptor like 'premium' is lazy and unhelpful. Both a memorable and a disappointing drink experience warrant a description based upon our sensory experiences. Only then might there be additional value in assessing whether the experience justifies premium pricing or not.

Many spirits are truly great products, some with origins that have helped to mould history itself. Many have existed for generations and some for centuries, distilled by families devoted to capturing the very best from their local environment. They are luxury purchases for most and so should be enjoyed, like wines, with passion, with knowledge, and through informed and entertaining recommendation.

3

MAKING COCKTAILS

Watching a bartender at work, standing in front of a dazzling array of polished bottles, surrounded by myriad spoons, tweezers, swizzle sticks and shakers, with a head full of almost arcane knowledge and grimoire-worthy catalogues of recipes, the process of creating a cocktail can seem hugely daunting. However their job relies on this mystique, even though, in reality, the art of creating great cocktails, if not simple, is much easier than some would have you believe.

When faced with any new challenge, whether it be computer coding or serving overarm the most important step is to reduce the problem into manageable chunks, the first principles on which any skill is founded. Often this requires stripping away the unnecessary, the half truths and sometimes downright lies surrounding the correct method, rather like a distiller removes the impurities and unwanted components from the first distillation.

At its most vodka-like in purity, mixology can be reduced to five simple to follow steps. Follow these and the results, although possibly lacking in the flair and elegance only obtainable through thousands of hours of practice, will surprise you, and delight your guests.

INGREDIENTS

'Put garbage in, get garbage out,' is a commonly repeated saying in many fields. Although many of the classic recipes produced in the speakeasy era were probably designed to mask the taste of poor quality liquor, it is true that better quality ingredients will produce a better quality final drink. Always use the best you can afford. One of the joys of making drinks at home is the fact that you can use ingredients that would be prohibitively expensive to drink in a bar.

Once you have purchased the ingredients, look after them. Plenty of home-bar liquor shelves are full of stale liqueurs, oxidized vermouths and dried up condiments. Where possible keep vermouth and other wine based products in the fridge to preserve them. Even then they will not last indefinitely and should be tasted and discarded if necessary before besmirching a cocktail. Fruit liqueurs, particularly cassis and framboise, are very prone to oxidation, losing their beautiful ruby colour and delicate aromas and fading to a dusty brown. Limiting oxidation with a wine saver will ensure longevity but if only a small amount of the product is required it is often worth sourcing a smaller package – most products are available as miniatures and these can often be the perfect solution.

Fresh ingredients – such as the fresh lime and lemon juice which form the backbone of whole categories of drinks – should be just that. They markedly deteriorate only hours after squeezing and so should be juiced as close to mixing as possible. Try to use fruits that are in season. Although modern grocery shopping has been transformed with the jet age, with everything from strawberries to lychees being available year round, cocktails that incorporate these types of fragrant and sweet produce always taste better when the fruit is ripe and in perfect condition.

The most important ingredient of all is ice, the use of which is vital to the very idea of the cocktail. You can never have too much ice, and again it should be of the very best quality. If making your own, the key to great ice is slow freezing. This allows air dissolved in the ice to dissipate during freezing, producing cubes that are crystal clear and slow to melt. Ideally Ice cubes should be just that, cubes, and with dimensions of at least an inch. Toroids, crescents and other shapes that can be commonly purchased are designed for quicker production but have the unfortunate side effect of melting much more quickly. As a guide, shaking a straight up cocktail like a Gin

Martini requires about six ounces of ice, while a shaken cocktail served over ice will require nearer to twelve. Always over supply as delicious drinks often require another to follow and any spare ice is great for keeping wine and sodas chilled before their inclusion in another drink.

RECIPES

A recipe is simply the ratio of the ingredients used to make the drink. There are countless cocktail books available, many with in excess of five-hundred recipes. If following one of these recipes the most important requirement is to measure the drink exactly. Measuring liquid ingredients requires precision and good instruments, ideally calibrated to all the measurements that are required. A good set of chef's measuring spoons should cover the smaller measurements but it is worth investing in some bartending spirit measures and pour spouts to help with accuracy.

The key to a great recipe is balance; each ingredient contributes to the levels of sweetness, acidity, bitterness, alcohol and aroma. Due to the very personal nature of people's appreciation of taste, most published recipes are written with a bias towards simplicity and pleasing to the middle of the road palate. Once you are confident with your ability to replicate a recipe accurately, it should be treated as a guide. Adapting a recipe slightly in response to your own or friends' taste to produce perfection is one of the true joys of mixology.

Bloody Mary, Dry Martini, Manhattan, Daiquiri … there is a list of drinks that everyone is familiar with, drinks you can order in any bar in the world and be reasonably confident you'll be presented with a respectable version. Due to their popularity, these drinks have become reference classics for the intrepid explorer into the world of spirits. Every category of spirits has these signature drinks and when assessing the quality of the spirit these reference drinks are very useful for comparison (reference recipes are found at the ends of chapters 4, 5, 6, 8, 9, 13 and 16). Having a personalized standard recipe for these drinks also allows you to investigate new products without having to buy a whole bottle, instead sampling them where you see them in a bar or restaurant.

There is a catechism that bartenders learn very early on. Two parts strong, one part weak, one part sour to one part sweet. This simple 2:1:1:1 ratio will create serviceable recipes with almost any ingredients and is a great place to start experimenting and to find your own particular appreciation of balance and harmony.

A NOTE ON BITTERS

Aromatic bitters have evolved from tinctures and patent medicines, gaining in popularity partly as they provide an excuse to have a drink. Their inclusion in recipes has become one of the defining features of a cocktail, as they stimulate rarely accessed areas of our palate with tastes that we are not normally conditioned to accept as pleasant. Bitterness works in concert with sourness to balance sugar and adds an extra dimension to any flavour combination. There are huge numbers of artisan bitters available now, based on different selections of aromatics. They can transform a cocktail and are very worthy of experimentation. Just remember to use in small quantities. It is easy to add more but impossible to take any away.

TEMPERATURE AND DILUTION

Choosing a good recipe and accurately measuring the ingredients require care but correct dilution and temperature manipulation, the most important parts of making a drink, require judgment. Ice chills the drink and adds water to the mixture at the same time. This water is a vital component of the drink, responsible for bringing the alcohol down to a more palatable level and providing space for the flavours to interact. Too much water, however, and the drink will become flat and lifeless, with too many aromatics lost from the spirit and too much loss of character from the sweet ingredients.

This requirement for controlled dilution is set against the desire to serve drinks at the correct temperature. The service temperature of spirits and wines plays a huge role in their flavour presentation.

Aromatic molecules evaporate faster and in different aggregate composition at higher temperatures, making profound changes to the profile of the liquid. There are recommended temperatures for serving different types of wine and beer ranging from 5 to 18°C. For cocktails the temperature is colder, sometimes much colder.

When making shaken drinks served over ice, the aim is to reduce the temperature of the liquid to close to freezing, so it can be poured over ice at nearly the same temperature. This prevents further dilution for the longest time, producing a drink that is consistent in flavour across its lifespan.

When making stirred or shaken drinks, served straight up, the ideal temperature is much colder – as low as -7°C – because, once in the glass, they will warm continuously. The colder the initial temperature, the longer the drink will remain pleasantly chilled.

To help make colder, more consistent drinks it is necessary to concentrate on your bar preparation. Keep ice in the freezer as long as possible. As soon as surface melt water appears on the ice, the melting process is accelerated and can easily contribute to over-dilution. Put all glassware for straight-up drinks in a freezer, if possible, for at least an hour before use. Cold glassware will help prevent changes in temperature. If possible, refrigerate other ingredients, particularly sodas and other ingredients used in large quantities in highballs. This will also preserve their carbonation.

THE PROCESS

The conversion of ingredients into the final drink involves, most obviously, mixing, chilling and diluting and, in the case of shaking, aeration. The simplest method is to stir over ice. This is normally performed in a Boston glass or speciality mixing glass. Stirring easily combines miscible ingredients and leaves a limpid finish without bubbles or ice in the finished drink. Due to the gentle nature of the process, it is possible to have close control over the dilution of the drink, ensuring that Martinis and Manhattans are not overly diluted. To improve thermal efficiency choose a heavyweight glass that allows for the use of lots of ice and ideally keep it in the freezer.

Shaking will effectively incorporate less-easy to mix ingredients like syrups and juices. Correctly performed it also adds significant amounts of air to the mixture, easily noted when making a shaken Martini because when first poured the drink will be opaque and full of tiny bubbles. These bubbles of air contain aromatic molecules from the spirit, popping and releasing flavour onto the palate. The air that's incorporated also lightens the texture of the drink. For this reason it is vital to serve drinks immediately after shaking, while they are still 'laughing at you'.

Cocktail shakers come in a number of shapes and sizes but can be divided into two main categories. Boston shakers consist of two conical pieces of either glass or steel. The two halves are held together during shaking by atmospheric pressure due to the decrease in volume of the chilled gases inside. For this reason they require a perfect fit to work effectively. When using the Boston shaker the correct amount of ice to use is governed by the size of the mixing half of the shaker set which should be filled to the brim. A 'standard' shaker consists of a mixing vessel, sometimes of a whimsical shape and a combination cap often with integrated strainer. When using a standard shaker two-thirds fill it with ice before capping.

Shake hard! The more the ice collides in the shaker, the more air that is incorporated and the more the ice cubes will begin to break, delivering faster rates of cooling and dilution, and the more the difficult ingredients and even fresh soft fruits will be incorporated. The length of time required shaking depends on the quality and temperature of the ice, but in general terms it should be around eight to ten seconds.

Vigorous shaking generates large numbers of ice fragments, necessitating the use of a strainer to remove them from the drink. For drinks served over ice this is less of a concern. A Hawthorne strainer will adequately remove enough of these shards and the rest will melt slower in the presence of the ice in the drinker's glass. When straining drinks that are to be served straight up it is often preferable to remove all of the shards and in this case the use of a fine mesh strainer will give a perfectly clean finish.

There is a distinct category of drinks that utilize an alternate method of chilling and dilution. Drinks like the Mint Julep and the Mojito are swizzled or churned. This involves rapidly agitating the drinks in the glass in which the drink is to be served, normally using crushed or cracked ice. These smaller ice shards melt much faster contributing a larger amount of water to the recipe. Recipes that benefit from this style of preparation often rely on this water to lengthen a cocktail, particularly when it is to be consumed in hot weather. Although swizzling can be performed with a spoon, a purpose made swizzle stick will enable faster, neater and less tiring presentation. After the required dilution has occurred and the ingredients are thoroughly mixed it is beneficial to top up the glass with dry crushed ice to help limit further melting.

PRESENTATION

The first 'sip' of any drink is with the eye. Looks matter. A visually appealing drink will taste better. Although the final appearance of a drink often relies on the last few steps of garnishing and service, presentation should be dealt with at the beginning of the process, ideally hours before the drinks are to be made.

There are two main elements: the glassware and the garnish. Glassware comes in a huge range of styles and sizes and correct choice depends on the style of drink to be served.

The traditional v-shaped cocktail glass is in many ways a limiting choice for cocktails made with aromatic spirits. Its complete absence of bowl means that evaporating flavour molecules quickly dissipate. These glasses do however allow for the use of citrus zest as a garnish, whereas in other styles of glassware this aroma can easily dominate. Try and choose glasses that fit the size of the recipe. It is recommended to have two sizes of glass for straight up drinks, with a 5.5oz glass for stirred spirituous drinks like a Manhattan and a larger 7.5–8.5oz glass for shaken drinks like a Daiquiri. Regardless of the shape or size, all straight up glassware should be kept in the freezer.

Drinks served on the rocks, or highballs can be served in a variety of tumblers and tall glasses. Short drinks like an Old Fashioned work best in a tumbler of around 9oz, while shaken drinks will benefit from a larger 12oz size. It is also desirable to have some larger, long glasses of 14oz and upwards for the service of cocktail highballs like a Tom Collins or tropical drinks.

The garnish of a drink plays an equal part in creating a pleasing appearance and often contributes directly to the flavour of a cocktail. There are no rules on what can be a successful garnish; the key to success is that they are prepared in advance. It is impossible to cut even the simplest lemon twist or lime wedge to the correct standard after the drink is created without the drink suffering by either warming up or becoming diluted. For this reason, the garnish should be the first thing that is approached, allowing care and attention to be devoted to it.

There are lots of specialist garnish preparation tools available, often in the pastry section of a kitchen supply shop. A canele cutter for cutting lengths of peel can be useful and, if you plan to make a lot of citrus zest garnish, a good peeler is worth borrowing from the kitchen but, for most applications, a sharp paring knife with about a 10cm blade will be sufficient.

Olives and onions, along with strawberries and other soft fruits are often used as garnish. They are there to be eaten and, to make this easier and so they can be consumed elegantly, it is always worthwhile serving them skewered on a cocktail stick. From experience it often makes sense to serve a few extras on the side, particularly with well-stuffed olives!

Chapters 4, 5, 6, 8, 9, 13 and 16 include a small selection of cocktails, most of them reference classics for each category. Each has comprehensive instructions to help reinforce the correct methodology. The drinks have been chosen to demonstrate the different characteristics of spirits and should bring many joyful hours of experimentation.

Bottoms up!

4

VODKA

BACKGROUND

When vodka first arrived in the west in the 1950s it was claimed to be tasteless and odourless. Indeed, the US government initially defined vodka as a clear, neutral spirit, distilled or treated after distillation with charcoal or other materials so as to be without discernible flavour or aroma. Smirnoff's earliest campaign in the west even claimed the vodka would 'leave you breathless'. Described by some at the time, as 'white whisky', vodka proved to be a successful iconoclast and rapidly became a hit with the young, but initially its heritage was ignored, which prevented recognition of its own product realities.

The EU now defines vodka as a spirit in which the organoleptic characteristics of the raw materials are selectively reduced: a definition that certainly describes more accurately many of the vodkas that emanate from the east and some of the more recent vodkas created in the west. Vodka remains the purest of spirits, but many now do retain certain characteristics from their raw materials.

Vodka is the world's most popular international spirit. Historically, it has usually been drunk neat in the east, a refuge from life's horrors, typically accompanied by food, and taken to help with the digestion of fatty foods. Here, vodka's usual consumption remains functional. But a generation of luxury sipping brands is now appealing to a growing number of affluent Polish and Russian consumers.

In the west, vodka has been drunk more as a lifestyle statement than because of what is in the bottle. So long as it was clean and neutral few had reason to know or care about vodka's product realities except perhaps for its alcoholic strength. The future looks very different, with westerners now calling for so-called 'vodkas with character', whether traditional vodkas from the east or one of the many vodkas with taste, texture and aromatics now distilled in the west.

HISTORY OF VODKA

The exact origins of vodka production remain uncertain, with Russians and Poles both claiming to have first distilled it in the Middle Ages. Knowledge of distillation spread from France and Northern Italy during the late thirteenth and early fourteenth centuries, so it could have reached Poland first, but neither Poland nor Russia has definitive evidence to support their claims.

Russia gave us the word *voda*, meaning 'water' and *vodka* meaning 'little water' though Poland has similar words: *woda* and *wodka*. The diminutive syllable *ka*, when used during the Middle Ages, meant 'better': a description that was very likely true of vodka because much water at that time not only tasted bad but could be very unhealthy, too.

Three copies of a Polish book dated 1405 contain mention of how to infuse wodka and a 1534 Polish scientific text includes a section on how to produce wodka, how to distil herb wodka, and suggesting how to use wodka to cleanse the skin after shaving or to rub on after a bath to remove unpleasant odours.

Initially, distilling wodka in Poland was the right only of aristocrats. But in 1546 King Jan Olbrecht issued a decree permitting every citizen to make it. Distillation became a family affair and a commercial opportunity for the merchant classes. In the sixteenth century, forty-nine commercial distilleries operated in the town of Poznan alone: a town that remains a major centre of wodka production. Early wodka was consumed more as medicine than as a social drink. Today's use of flavourings like bison grass, still found in Zubrowka, reflects this history. Aged wodka was also a tradition in the Polish–Lithuanian Commonwealth. At a child's birth the father would pour homemade wodka into an empty oak barrel, previously used to store wine. The barrel was sealed and buried, ready to be dug up and served as the toast at the child's wedding banquet.

The claim that Russians first distilled vodka stems from a fourteenth century visit to a Russian prince by a delegation from Genoa, one of the earliest centres of distilling. Later, a Russian delegation visited Northern Italy and returned to Moscow with sufficient knowledge to start distilling vodka. The early distillates were most likely used for medicine or even gunpowder.

A century later a monopoly on the sale and distillation of spirits was imposed in Moscow, suggesting that consumption by then had already become considerable. In the 1540s, the Russian Tsar Ivan the Terrible established his own network of distilling taverns to ensure that profits went straight into the Imperial Treasury. Initially he outlawed all taverns that were outside his control but later, looking to increase his income, the tsar sold licenses to the nobility. The spirit produced at this time was full of impurities and aggressive in character so honey and other ingredients were added to make it palatable.

From the seventeenth century, however, vodka was consumed for social and medicinal reasons. It became customary for it to be served at Russian Imperial banquets. All formal meals began with bread and vodka. The Governor of Moscow trained a large bear to serve pepper vodka to his guests. If any guest refused their drink, the bear removed their clothes. Vodka was also drunk at religious festivals. Peter the Great was renowned for his hospitality and love of drinking which encouraged him to take an interest in the distillation process. He visited the Netherlands, then at the cutting edge of distilling knowledge, and brought back new technical insights for the Russian distillers to adopt in the eighteenth century.

Successive rulers maintained their monopoly on vodka distillation while continuing to grant distilling rights to the nobility and to government officials. In 1863, however, the monopoly on distilling in Russia was repealed and private companies were allowed to produce vodka.

This encouraged Pyotr Smirnov, among others, to set up his distillery in Moscow. Until then vodkas had remained far from pure: the product of single or double pot distillation to only low levels of alcohol. But the Smirnov family pioneered charcoal filtration and, in the 1870s, they were among the first in Russia to use the continuous distillation process. This process made it possible to remove many impurities and the spirit became increasingly palatable without the addition of flavourings.

However, to assist the war effort, distillation of vodka was banned in Russia in 1914. Only three years later, in 1917, the masses, who were no longer drunk, rebelled and overthrew the government, no doubt encouraging Stalin to rediscover the benefit the tsars had seen in ensuring supplies of cheap vodka during his subsequent reign of terror.

The Smirnov family fled the Russian Revolution, changed its name to Smirnoff and set up in Europe, but without success. The family sold its recipe to a friend, Rudolph Kunett with whom they had traded in Moscow and who had escaped to America. He introduced Smirnoff there in 1934. His efforts were not successful but, during World War II, western troops had enjoyed drinking vodka with Russian soldiers, making them a ready market when Heublein, the company to whom Kunett had sold the recipe, launched the Smirnoff 'breathless' revolution in the 1950s.

In Sweden, the tradition of distilling vodka dates from the fifteenth century, but it was a distilling prodigy named Lars Olsson Smith who introduced continuous distillation and, in the nineteenth century, began to distil spirits with very low levels of impurities. His fame grew, particularly for Absolut Rent Brännvin, when it was launched in 1879, and his success earned him the local title of 'King of Spirits'. Vodka, however, failed to gain any broad success across Western Europe until the latter half of the twentieth century, significantly assisted by the Swedish monopoly's launch of Absolut Vodka in 1979. All Absolut vodka continues to be produced in Åhus.

In the twenty-first century, vodka has consolidated its position as the world's best-selling international spirit. In traditional eastern markets, fashion brands have taken a share of sales, while in the west vodkas continue to provide the neutral base for long, mixed drinks. However, those capturing market share in the west now offer heritage, provenance and character in the bottle, whether sourced from the water, the raw materials or the production process.

RAW MATERIALS

According to EU regulations, vodka is a spirit produced from ethyl alcohol of agricultural origin. Traditionally, this has usually meant grain or potatoes, raw materials that contain starches rather than sugars. To convert these starches into fermentable sugars, the grain or potatoes must first be cooked. Commercial enzymes are then added to stimulate the conversion process. Nowadays, fruits and molasses are also used and their existing sugars mean they do not require conversion.

Whatever the process, once a sugary liquid does exist, yeasts are added to stimulate fermentation and convert the sugars into a low alcohol wash of around 8% to 10%. This wash is then distilled and rectified to selectively reduce the organoleptic characteristics of the raw materials and the by-products formed during fermentation. The process involves multiple distillations and may be followed by filtration either to polish or to eliminate any remaining character.

Though price can influence the choice, for example, between molasses and wheat, the relative alcohol yield can also affect the decision to use one ingredient versus another. Historically, however, the choice usually depended on what the local environment provided, meaning grain and potatoes in Europe, molasses in the Caribbean, corn in America and, more recently, grapes in wine producing countries. In 2008, the EU Parliament rejected a proposal by Poland, Finland, the Baltic States, Sweden and Denmark to tighten the legal definition of vodka.

These countries wanted vodka to be defined as a spirit made only from potatoes or grain. The EU did not agree but did specify that vodka made from anything other than potatoes or cereals should carry the words 'produced from' supplemented by the name of the raw material(s) used to produce the ethyl alcohol. Even though the finished spirit must be distilled to high levels of alcohol distillers can choose to produce vodkas that are pure and yet still retain some of the quality and character of their raw materials.

Wheat is the raw material used for most vodkas produced outside Poland. The preference is for winter wheat (rather than summer wheat) sown in the autumn and harvested in the following late summer or autumn; the longer cultivation cycle ensures the wheat contains more starch. This starch quantity determines the alcohol yield. Wheat starches are efficiently converted into sugars and wheat tends to generate a creamy style of vodka with distinct notes of aniseed.

Rye is the grain used extensively in Poland. Rye provides sweet, slightly nutty, rye bread-like notes with possible hints of pepper on the finish and an oily texture on the palate.

Potatoes are not indigenous to Europe; they were introduced in the sixteenth century and were first used for vodka production in Poland during the nineteenth century. Special high starch varieties are traditionally cultivated for vodka production in specific microclimates such as along the river Vistula as well as on the Baltic coast. They are a more costly option than grain because their preparation is labour-intensive and they produce only around 30% of the level of spirit generated by a comparable quantity of grain. They produce vodkas that are full-bodied, rich in style and full of mashed potato character.

Maize/corn is used in America, where it is the native grain. When its price is low corn may also be the choice elsewhere in place of wheat. Corn delivers real buttery notes, reminiscent of corn on the cob.

Six-row barley is indigenous to Finland and is different to the two-row barley cultivated in the rest of the world. Yielding low levels of fatty oils, this barley contributes a clean and soft grainy character that is slightly dry and nutty.

Mixed grains are a recent introduction. Sometimes the grains are even mixed with potatoes. The skill of the distiller is to capture and enhance the best of each ingredient.

Molasses, obtained from sugar cane, is the usual choice in the Caribbean. But sugar beet may be used elsewhere because it is cheaper than grain and cost can be a factor in production. Molasses tend to yield a distinct sweetness on the palate.

Grapes are a relatively recent raw material used in the production of vodka. They tend to retain more flavour and aroma than grain when rectified, resulting in a richly textured, highly aromatic vodka, distinctively fruity and fresh.

Water is a crucial ingredient. Its source is increasingly promoted as part of a brand's credentials. According to a Polish saying, 'water breathes life into vodka'. It is used to cook the raw materials and to reduce the alcohol strength prior to bottling. Water can account for as much as 62.5% of the bottled vodka so differing water sources, whether glacial, spring or mineral can deliver significant variations even between vodkas distilled from the same raw materials. However, water's real contribution must be distinguished from what marketing may sometimes claim. Prior to use, any potential contribution from the water may be reduced through deionization and filtration, two processes that remove calcium ions and other hard minerals. Any minerals remaining in the water are noticeable in the finished vodka either in taste or by throwing a haze in the bottle.

PRODUCTION OF VODKA

Milling or shredding of the ingredients increases their surface area and optimizes the process of breaking down the starch cell walls prior to their conversion. Conversion is the process of transforming the starches into fermentable sugars by cooking the ingredients in hot water and releasing or adding enzymes. Fermentation is the process of adding yeast to convert this liquid, full of fermentable sugars, into alcohol. The fermented liquid, known as the 'wash', has an alcoholic strength of around 8%–10% ABV. The wash not only contains ethanol but also flavour compounds such as esters, aldehydes, acids and fusel oils, otherwise called congeners. Rapid fermentation must be avoided if sugars or yeasts are not to be left in the wash to burn during distillation.

Pot stills were the only stills available for production of early vodkas so they retained considerable character from their raw materials. Some distillers still choose to use pot stills to retain character or to refine the final distillate.

Column stills are the more usual choice of today's vodka distillers because they can run at much higher temperatures and permit the distiller to be very precise in the elimination and retention of distillates. A varying number of plates, some perforated and others not, are fitted in the rectifier to eliminate or capture specific alcohols and the character of a vodka will vary significantly according to the number and location of plates fitted.

Rectification is the process of passing the spirit through a number of columns to remove all impurities and to raise the alcoholic strength to at least 96% ABV. Single, or more usually double distillation, may be sufficient when spirits are able to mellow during years in wood but rectification is required to remove much more from a spirit that rarely enjoys any maturation and yet prides itself on its purity and smoothness; the greater the number of columns through which a distillate passes, the greater the elimination of congeners and the more neutral the character of the finished vodka. After distillation, vodkas may be filtered before dilution to the required strength.

Filtration can be used either to influence the taste or to 'polish' the vodka. A mesh filter is used to polish the distillate, preventing fine particles or sediment from passing through the bottling line. Charcoal is one of the most common materials used to modify the character of the vodka, particularly charcoal made from hard woods such as silver birch. Charcoal is very absorbent, especially when activated (see Principles of distillation). Some producers tip charcoal into holding tanks to absorb impurities as it descends through the distillate. Others pump the spirit through numerous columns, packed with charcoal, taking considerable time for it to exit through a final membrane filter.

Quartz sand is another popular filter medium but a large number of other mediums are also used: some probably more for their marketing value than for their filtration benefits. It is important to evaluate whether filters are used primarily to purify, to polish or to help to market the vodka.

THE DIFFERENT STYLES OF VODKA

Many vodkas today are neutral in taste to provide the ideal base for mixed drinks but some, the vodkas with character, deliver tastes and aromas beyond the character of the alcohol itself. Though not neutral, the best of these still rightly pride themselves on their purity. There are no industry standards for vodka that can imply quality through letters or marks on the label. Instead, vodka brand names offer the promise of a consistent product, supported sometimes by reference to country of origin, or to the use of specific raw materials or production processes. These can all provide clues to a vodka's likely character but, even then, much will depend upon the nature of filtration.

Western style/neutral vodkas

Initially all, and still most, western vodkas are rectified spirits, distilled from grain or molasses and filtered: the more expensive through tons of charcoal and others, more crudely. They are then reduced with pure demineralized water and bottled, ready to drink, with no maturation, to be judged on their purity and cleanliness alone. They are simply pure ethanol and water. Style not substance, packaging not content may be the keys to the success of some, though others will rightly claim their success to be underpinned by exceptional purity, combined or not with texture. Neutral vodka is sufficiently light and crisp not to overwhelm any added mixer and remains the west's dominant choice

Vodkas with character

These will include eastern rye, wheat and potato vodkas that, thanks to modern distillation techniques, are now pure and clean, unlike their ancestors, but still retain some of the character of their raw material because their distillates were not distilled to neutral levels of alcohol. Some may also use herbs and spices or regional ingredients such as the fragrant bison grass or wild bees' honey in Poland. The traditions are strong and the flavours result from lengthy processes such as infusion and percolation. They are not the result of cold compounding (see Gin) as may be the case with some of today's so-called flavoured vodkas.

Today, vodkas with character certainly include some produced in the west. The companies making these are keen to differentiate them from neutral vodkas, claiming that their distillation process or the character retained from single or multiple grain formulae, potatoes or fruit carries through into the finished vodka either in terms of taste or texture or both. Consequently, the division between neutral vodkas from the west and character vodkas from the east no longer applies.

Flavoured vodkas

Flavoured vodka has been given a predominant flavour other than that derived from the raw materials. The vodka may be sweetened, blended, flavoured, matured or coloured. Poland and Russia produce the largest range and, initially at least, these vodkas were flavoured to mask the raw nature of the alcohol.

Traditionally, the ingredients were macerated in the spirit for varying periods of time. Today, flavoured vodkas may result from cold compounding with extracts or natural ingredients that have been macerated in alcohol and/or water. They may result from percolation or from flavoured distillates being blended in before bottling. Some may be little more than simple brand extensions while others are the result of complex recipes.

Aged vodkas

Ageing vodka is a traditional approach which has been used in Poland and Russia since the sixteenth century.

VODKA CONSUMPTION

High alcohol spirits like vodka remain liquid even in very cold temperatures, making them particularly attractive in northern countries. In Russia, vodka is traditionally drunk chilled or frozen and downed in one. The Russians shoot rather than sip partly because of a belief that it is the fumes going up the nose, rather than the liquid itself, that causes drunkenness.

In Poland, vodka is typically sipped, with food and at room temperature to allow the tastes and aromas to be enjoyed.

In the west, vodka has gained its popularity as a neutral spirit, mixed with fruit juices or in cocktails. But today, knowing more about the raw materials, appreciating the influence of production processes on what is in the bottle and discovering the heritage and traditions of vodka are as important to the enjoyment of this spirit as to any other.

Quiz on vodka

1. Which Russian scientist determined 38% ABV to be vodka's ideal alcohol content?

    A. Pyotr Smirnov
    B. Boris Nikolsky
    C. Rudolf Kunett
    D. Dmitri Mendeleev

2 What is the predominant method of distillation used to produce vodka?

A. Pot distillation
B. Carter Head distillation
C. Vapour distillation
D. Column distillation

3 What is the literal meaning of the words 'vodka' and 'wodka'?

A. White water
B. Little water
C. Clean water
D. Cold water

4. Which is the main grain used to produce Polish vodka?

A. Wheat
B. Corn
C. Barley
D. Rye

5. Which of the following ingredients is typically used to produce Russian vodka?

A. Wheat
B. Potato
C. Barley
D. Rye

6. In which year was the state monopoly on distilling in Russia repealed?

A. 1849
B. 1851
C. 1863
D. 1874

7. Smirnoff vodka was first distilled in which town?

    A. Harlow, England
    B. Moscow, Russia
    C. Krakow, Poland
    D. Hartford CT, USA

8. Which of these Polish vodkas is flavoured with bison grass?

    A. Zubrowka
    B. Wisniowka
    C. Wyborowa
    D. Luksusowa

9. Every bottle of Absolut vodka is distilled in which town in Sweden?

    A. Stockholm
    B. Åhus
    C. Orebro
    D. Gothenburg

10. When did Smirnoff vodka arrive in the USA?

    A. 1961
    B. 1953
    C. 1934
    D. 1914

11. Whose local success earned him the title 'King of Spirits' in the late nineteenth century?

    A. Pyotr Smirnov
    B. Jack Martin
    C. Lars Olsson Smith
    D. Rudolf Kunett

12. Which of these raw materials would typically generate hints of aniseed in a vodka?

    A. Corn
    B. Potatoes
    C. Rye
    D. Wheat

13. To be classified as rectified and neutral, a spirit must exceed what level of alcohol?

    A. 92% ABV
    B. 94% ABV
    C. 96% ABV
    D. 98% ABV

14. By what century did vodka production become a commercial practice in Poland?

    A. Fifteenth
    B. Sixteenth
    C. Seventeenth
    D. Eighteenth

15. In which country, in microclimates on the banks of the river Vistula, are potatoes cultivated for vodka production?

    A. Poland
    B. Russia
    C. Finland
    D. Bulgaria

16. Today, which of the early centres of distillation in Poland remains a major town for wodka production?

    A. Gdansk
    B. Poznan
    C. Krakow
    D. Nowy Sacz

17. Which Russian ruler visited the Netherlands to learn more about distillation?

   A. Ivan the Terrible
   B. Catherine the Great
   C. Peter the Great
   D. Nicholas II

18. Which of these raw materials is generally the most costly to use in vodka production?

   A. Corn
   B. Rye
   C. Wheat
   D. Potato

MAKING COCKTAILS WITH VODKA

Vodka did not become popular beyond the countries of production until after the Second World War, when its speed of production and relatively cheap price made it one of the only spirits readily available to the masses. Since it was originally marketed as a spirit without flavour, bartenders jumped at their chance to work with a blank canvas, particularly using a whole new set of ingredients made possible by the technological advances in food processing and storage that came about due to the conflict.

When served neat or in a very dry Vodka Martini it is possible to discern the differences in taste and flavour between brands, and note characteristics inherited from the various raw materials and methods of production. However in most cocktails, particularly the 'fruit based drinks' category which vodka dominates, most of vodka's nuances of flavour and texture are lost. When buying vodka therefore it is wise to think of its usage first. A standard brand, as long as it is 40% abv (eighty proof) will be sufficient for all but the most spirit heavy cocktails.

The Bloody Mary

To many people the idea of a savoury cocktail means only one thing: the Bloody Mary. Created by Fernand 'Pete' Petiot in 1921 in The New York Bar in Paris, the original recipe was an adaptation of simpler, unspiced, tomato juice drinks. He added a fair amount of salt, pepper, cayenne, lemon juice and of course Worcestershire sauce. Although unknown at the time, several of the ingredients in Worcestershire sauce, particularly the fermented anchovy, contain large amounts of glutamic acid, which we now recognize as one of the sources of the fifth taste – umami. This particular savoury taste is what makes the drink so satisfying and moreish, particularly as tomatoes also stimulate umami receptors, and their thickness allows for a level of seasoning not possible with other ingredients.

50ml vodka
5ml lemon juice
5 drops Tabasco
5 dashes Worcestershire sauce
small pinch of salt
3 grinds white pepper
170ml tomato juice

Place all ingredients into a large mixing glass and stir gently with ice. If you shake tomato juice it will begin to separate and form a scum. Try hard to find fresh pressed tomato juice as the flavour and texture is far more pleasant than that from concentrate and ambient storable juice. Strain over ice into a large highball glass and garnish with a lemon wedge and a stick of celery.

One of the best things about a Bloody Mary is perfecting your own recipe. Horseradish, wasabi, balsamic vinegar, dry sherry, red wine, homemade hot sauce, beef bouillon, carrot juice; the list of additions and modifications is almost endless. If serving Bloody Marys for a group at brunch, perhaps provide a simple mix and allow guests to experiment, making personalized drinks with their favourites chosen from an array of ingredients and condiments.

Vodka Espresso

Commonly known as an Espresso Martini, the Vodka Espresso was created by the late, great Dick Bradsell, the guiding force behind much of the UK's modern cocktail renaissance. Tasked with making a drink to revive flagging partygoers, he used ristretto espresso coffee allied with coffee liqueur and a healthy slug of vodka and served it short and strong.

The drink became an almost instant modern classic, riding the wave of new cocktail bars alongside the parallel resurgence of the craft coffee scene to become a menu stalwart of bars across the world. Indeed it is regularly the best selling of all cocktails in bars where it is available.

40ml vodka
10ml Kahlua
10ml Toussaint
1 ristretto espresso

Place all the ingredients apart from the coffee in a cocktail shaker. Prepare the espresso with an extra firm tamp, compressing the ground coffee further to decrease the speed of extraction, and cut off the flow promptly to create a ristretto. Add the coffee to the shaker and quickly and firmly shake, remembering that the hot coffee will lead to higher than normal dilution. Strain into a chilled cocktail glass; a well-made Espresso should resemble a Guinness when it is poured, the crema from the coffee having expanded to hold lots of air. Garnish with three coffee beans (con mosca) for luck.

Toussaint can be difficult to get hold of so you can substitute any fairly dry coffee liqueur or just use Kahlua, although Kahlua is quite sweet. If you take your coffee with sugar you might find a dash of simple syrup (see page 95) before shaking makes a drink even more to your taste. The contribution of vodka to the taste of this drink is masked by the strong flavours of coffee but the vodka can certainly contribute to texture. So try using a creamy wheat vodka to produce a drink that goes down even more easily.

Vodka Martini

The Vodka Martini has benefitted from the sponsorship of a certain secret agent. The drink which Ian Fleming named the Vesper in his first James Bond book, *Casino Royale*, is actually made with a combination of gin and vodka. Unfortunately the Vesper as written uses a product no longer available, Kina Lillet, so we will never know if Bond was a great mixologist along with all his other skills.

At its finest the dry Vodka Martini can be an amazing drink, really showcasing the quality and character of the vodka used. Russian vodka will produce a peppery and intense version with a shorter finish whereas Swedish and other Scandinavian vodkas will make a smoother drink with a rounder mouthfeel and longer finish.

Just as there are many variations of the Gin Martini, the choice of modifying ingredient, the proportions and garnish can be changed in a Vodka Martini to create a whole series of similarly delicious but subtly different cocktails. The Golden Gibson below is one of the very best.

The Golden Gibson substitutes dry vermouth with another herbal ingredient, in this case the monastery liqueur Benedictine. This high proof liqueur has notes of honey and alpine herbs, many of which are found in vermouth. Its sweetness pairs well with very chilled spirit, amplifying the flavours. To balance this with both an acidic bite and textural crunch, garnish the drink with pickled onions.

The Golden Gibson

60ml best quality vodka
10ml Benedictine

Stir the ingredients with ice in a large mixing glass – for the very coldest drink a vacuum flask works best. Just make sure the flask is one lined with steel! When bitingly cold strain into a chilled martini glass and garnish.

To make the golden onions add to pickling vinegar a pinch of sugar, turmeric, a few strands of saffron and small silverskin onions. They will quickly pick up a lovely golden colour and a hint of spice. When garnishing, serve as many onions as there are sips in the glass and, because they are so delicious, a few more on the side always go down well.

5

TEQUILA

WHAT IS TEQUILA?

Tequila is a spirit unique to Mexico. It is made from the blue agave, which is not a cactus but a member of the lily family. It must be produced only in strictly demarcated areas of Mexico. Historically, tequilas were bottled young but many are now aged. Most are natural but some are flavoured. Some are inexpensive while others can be very costly.

The following regulations, established by the Mexican government, define and control production of tequila. The spirit must be distilled only or primarily from the fermented juice of the blue agave, Agave tequilana Weber. When using sugars obtained only from the blue agave, the label states '100% agave' or '100% blue agave'. In the case of bottles labeled simply 'tequila', regulations allow for 51% of sugars to come from the juice of the blue agave with the remaining sugars coming from non-agave products, usually from sugar cane, which grows in Mexico.

Tequila must be distilled at least twice and must be produced only in the five demarcated regions of Mexico. Of all tequila, 99% is made in the state of Jalisco, where the town of Tequila is situated. The other regions include areas in the states of Guanajuato, Michoacan, Nayarit and Tamaulipas.

Tequila must be produced under the supervision of the Tequila Regulatory Council, set up in 1994, to oversee production in every distillery and to award certificates of quality, represented on labels by the initials CRT.

Authentic tequila, regulated in this way, will also carry a Norma Oficial Mexicana, or NOM, number on its label to identify the producing company. It also guarantees that the tequila is produced in accordance with regulations set by the Consejo Regulador del Tequila. Each distillery is given its own NOM number and all brands produced by that distillery will have the same number. This number is not a guarantee of quality, merely of authenticity.

In 1974, tequila gained global recognition as a product exclusive to Mexico, *hecho en Mexico* (made in Mexico), and produced according to these strict regulations.

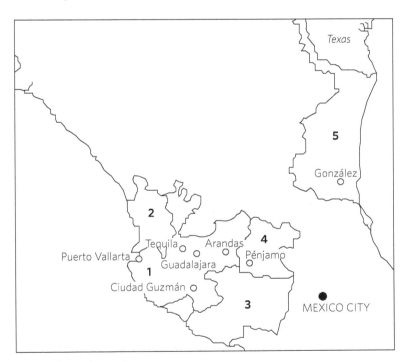

Map of tequila production areas

The town of Tequila, founded by the Spanish in 1530, lies in a high valley at the foot of Mount Tequila, 4,000 feet above sea level, just north of Guadalajara. To the east and beyond Guadalajara lie the so-called Highlands or Los Altos. These rise another 600 to 900 metres above Tequila valley. Here, the iron-rich volcanic soils, hot days and cool nights tend to produce agave that are bigger and sweeter than those in Tequila valley. Tequilas from here can be more citrusy and less earthy than those produced around Tequila town, in the valley. Los Altos now produces more tequila than Tequila valley.

HISTORY OF TEQUILA

Tequila's historical roots go back to pre-Columbian Mexican–Indian culture. When Cortez and his Spanish explorers arrived they found Indians drinking a ceremonial beverage called *pulque*, a drink of 3%–5% ABV, made from the fermented, sweet and milky sap of the agave. In Mexico today pulque continues to be consumed though it is being rapidly replaced by beer.

The Spaniards, looking for stronger alcohol, applied their distilling knowledge to the agave plant and came up with mezcal wine (agave is also known as mezcal). The first mention of this mezcal wine appeared around 1550.

By the 1700s, the distilled mezcal wine from a region situated around the village of Tequila was recognized as the best. In 1795, the first commercial licence to produce agave wine was granted there to José Maria Guadalupe de Cuervo. Others followed during the nineteenth century, including Don Cenobio Sauza, who established La Perseverancia Distillery in 1873, and began to transform this cottage craft into a commercial industry. Around 1850, the name tequila was widely used to describe the superior mezcal from this area.

Until the early 1900s, tequila production was small-scale and, as with any other mezcal, many different agave plants were used. By this time, however, the blue agave was widely known to deliver superior mezcal, even though then, as now, it was always difficult to adjust the planting of new agave to the changing levels of demand because the agave plant takes eight years or more to mature.

To ease this problem of supply and demand, in the 1930s a new style was created. It was then called 'mixto' but is now called tequila. This combines sugars from the blue agave with sugars from other non-agave sources like sugar cane. This mixture was softer in character and more appealing to the American palate. It remains the style of tequila most widely consumed in major export markets such as America, which is still tequila's most important customer.

During the first half of the twentieth century, tequila was a drink for non-conforming adventurers. Later, in the 1950s, a cocktail named the Margarita became popular in the Los Angeles area, expanding awareness and demand. Tequila became a mainstream choice and by the 1980s designer/boutique tequilas had caught the public's attention. Specially aged and packaged tequilas had existed before but these newcomers were now marketed as 100% blue agave tequilas and they were usually produced in limited quantities. The image of tequila became one of quality and exclusivity. People began to sip and savour their tequilas as well as to enjoy the character that tequila added to their mixed drinks.

Just as other spirits now enjoy individual recognition, so tequila is now recognized as a unique mezcal: the exclusive product of Mexico, distilled by scarcely 100 registered producers in around sixty distilleries, many of which are very modest affairs.

PRODUCTION

The blue agave

There are more than 200 varieties of agave in Mexico alone, but the species that must be used in tequila production is the Weber blue agave, which is sufficiently large and numerous to cast a blue hue across the volcanic landscape where it is grown. The agave flowers and bears fruit only once before dying. Fully matured, the leaves can reach shoulder height. Some, but not all, agave farmers prune the plants to encourage growth in the *piñas*, the name given to the heart of the plant and to reduce the risk of injury to harvesters from the strong, sharp spikes on the ends of the leaves.

Harvesting agave

Production begins with the *hijuelo*, the offshoot or offspring produced by the parent plant. This is separated from the base and replanted in rows similar to vines but further apart to accommodate the size of the plant when fully grown. Though trials are in progress to shorten the time to maturity to nearer five years, plants are generally left unattended for seven to twelve years until maturation.

Harvesting agave

At an average age of eight to nine years, the plant is ready to harvest, containing sufficient starch for conversion into the sugars needed to create alcohol. Growers must harvest the agave or cut off the *quiote*, or flowering shoot, before its flower begins to feed on the starches stored within the piña. Even though a field of agaves may be planted at the same time, each plant will reach maturity at a different time. This means that harvesting is a year-round activity except during the short rainy season.

Only the experience of skilled *jimadors* ensures that the harvesting of each plant is done at the right time. The *jimador* uses centuries-old tools to manually uproot and to trim a mature agave in about six minutes.

First, the sharp leaves are cut away as close as possible to the *piña* to avoid their bitterness transferring into the spirit. Then the *piña* is cut from its shallow roots. The heart weighs between twenty and fifty kilos, and resembles a large pineapple which is why it is called a *piña* in Mexico. The harvested *piñas* are transported to the distillery where they are halved or quartered before they are steam cooked.

Extraction of sugars

*Cooking agave (a) traditional oven (*horno*); (b) stainless steel autoclave*

The agave is steam cooked to convert its starches into fermentable sugars. The decision to cook slowly in traditional ovens or more quickly in autoclaves does affect the taste of the tequila. Traditional ovens or *hornos* are made from brick, stone, or mud and straw. But most distilleries now use the quicker system of pressure cooking up to sixty tons of agave in one batch, at high temperatures in stainless steel cylinders called autoclaves.

After cooking, the *piñas* are left to cool. Traditionally, the fibres are then transferred to a pit to be crushed by a stone wheel, called a *tahona*. This weighs as much as two tons and rotates round a pit pulled by a donkey or a tractor to crush out the sugary sap called *agua miel* or 'honey water'.

Crushing piñas with a tahona

Some distillers use modern steel crushing machines and jets of pressurized water to wash the sap out of the pulp.

Fermentation

The *agua miel* is transferred to stainless steel or wooden tanks and yeast is added to start the fermentation process. Commercial yeasts and accelerator enzymes are sometimes used to reduce the fermentation time. But if left to ferment only with natural yeasts, this process can take from ten to twelve days. Fermentation results in a liquid called *mosto muerto* or 'dead must' which has a low alcohol strength of around 5%–6% ABV.

Distillation

A few tequilas are triple distilled. Some are produced in column stills. But the tradition is to double distill the *mosto* in pot stills, which historically were made from copper but are now more usually constructed from stainless steel with a few copper panels inserted.

Heads and tails are removed after the first distillation though a proportion may be returned to the next run. The heart of the distillate is retained and called *ordinario*. Only when the *ordinario* has been distilled a second time and the heads and tails have been removed again can the distillate be called tequila. The alcohol strength of tequila that exits the column still or second pot still is not regulated. Only when commercialized as tequila must the strength lie between 35% and 55% ABV. Some, however, may distil to bottling strength.

Maturation

White or silver tequilas can be reduced with water and bottled straight from the still or rested for up to two months in stainless steel or wood. Tequila may be classified as aged only after resting for more than two months, in small barrels or large oak vats (see classifications below). Most will rest rather than mature, for no more than a few weeks to a year. Wood may be new or used, French or American oak, charred or toasted and the container may be a barrel holding as little as 200 litres or a large vat holding thousands of litres (see below the requirements of each specific classification). The choice of wood and time spent in ageing will influence the surprisingly delicate character of the agave so great care must be taken to ensure that the wood complements rather than overwhelms the character of the tequila itself.

TEQUILAS ARE NOT ALL THE SAME

The following are factors that can contribute to the various styles of tequila:

- The terroir or soil and climate where the agave is grown.

- The maturity of the agave plant.

- The nature of the oven and level of heat used to cook the *piña*.

- The time allowed for cooking and cooling.

- The water used to rinse the cooked, crushed agave and to dilute the spirit for bottling.

- Whether the yeast used to begin fermentation of the agave juice is natural or artificial.

- The distillation process, size and type of still used, duration of distillation and temperature set.

- The maturation time, size of container and nature of wood or other material used.

- The decision to make 100% agave tequila or regular tequila.

TEQUILA CLASSIFICATIONS

Tequila is usually bottled at 38% or 40% ABV. The following are the terms used to describe the different classes:

Silver/blanco/plata/white This style is often clear and full of the raw, vegetal character of the agave because it is not usually rested for any time. However, an increasing number are rested in wood, usually for thirty to forty-five days. The regulations permit no more than sixty days. This process mellows the overall character rather than extracting any significant contribution from the wood except maybe a hint of colour.

Gold/joven aboçado This is a white tequila coloured with caramel. If the description *reposado* is on the label, the tequila will also have been aged for at least two months.

Reposado This style was introduced in 1974 and today it is the most popular type of tequila in Mexico. This tequila must be aged in small oak casks or large oak vats holding as many as 20,000 litres, depending on whether only oxidation or the absorption of some wood character is required. The maturation time must exceed sixty days and invariably some of the fresh agave character is sacrificed to the wood. Caramel can be added for extra colour.

Añejo This tequila must be aged in government-sealed oak barrels holding no more than 600 litres for at least one year. Typically, the barrels are ex-bourbon casks of less than 200 litres.

Muy añejo/extra añejo This is a recent introduction for tequilas aged for at least three years, in oak barrels holding no more than 600 litres.

THREE WAYS TO CONSUME TEQUILA

- **Shot** Traditionally this was done with the ritual lick of salt, a shot of tequila and a bite of lime or lemon. In its extreme, this is done in a form called 'slamming', mixing the tequila with a carbonated beverage, banging the shot glass on a hard surface and consuming the drink in the fastest possible time. Young and/or inexpensive tequila is best for this style of drinking.

- **Cocktail** Cocktails are usually made with young tequilas, but increasingly the choice may be reposado or añejo and 100% agave tequilas (see page 73 for recipes).

- **Sip and savour** This is the way to enjoy 100% reposado and añejo tequilas, often from a brandy snifter or tasting glass to enhance the experience.

THE FUTURE OF TEQUILA

Marketing will continue to play an important role in accentuating and/or creating perceived differences amongst tequila brands and classes. To accomplish this, tequila will follow the example of other alcoholic spirits and borrow ideas, such as using vintages, creating more specific regional classifications, using different ways to age the product, and highlighting the use of traditional as opposed to mass means of production.

Tequila classified as 100% blue agave will continue to grow in popularity as consumers become more educated about tequila and more discriminating in their choices. However, it is unlikely that aged tequila will take over from *blanco* as, for many, the raw, vegetal nature of agave is all too easily overwhelmed after only a relatively short time in wood.

MEZCAL

In general, mezcal tastes more pungent and assertive than tequila. Regulations that pertain to mezcal production were written into the Norma Oficial Mexicana (NOM) in 1994 but not enacted until 2005 when Comercam, Consejo Mexicano Regulador de la Calidad del Mezcal, the Mezcal Regulatory Council, became operational. Since that date all certified mezcal carries a NOM number on its label. All mezcal must be bottled at point of origin and may not be shipped out of the country in bulk as is permitted with regular tequila.

Mezcal will sometimes be bottled *con gusano,* meaning containing the larva of a moth (not a worm) that lives on the agave plant, either on its leaves or in its roots. (These caterpillars are also eaten fried or dried and ground up with dried chillies and salt to sprinkle over food.)

Unlike tequila, mezcal can be produced from any of some thirty varieties of agave, including the blue agave. However the agave plants must be grown within the five states of Durango, Guerrero, Oaxaca, San Luis Potosí and Zacatecas or in limited areas within the states of Guanajuato and Tamaulipas. Today, there are around 9,000 agave producers and more than 600 distilleries, though Oaxaca accounts for as many as 90% of all the production facilities. Over six million litres are produced annually for more than 150 brands.

MEZCAL CLASSIFICATIONS

There are two styles, determined by percentage of agave:

• Mezcal, usually produced in small quantities, from 100% agave sugars.

• Mezcal distilled from at least 80% agave sugars.

There are five classifications relating to maturation:

Aboçado This term indicates that the spirit is bottled immediately after distillation and is sometimes enhanced with the addition of one or more flavouring or colouring agents.

Joven/blanco These terms imply that the spirit is either unaged or that it's been rested for less than two months.

Reposado This term confirms that the spirit has been rested for more than two months in wooden barrels or vats no larger than 200 litres.

Añejo This term confirms the spirit has been aged for at least twelve months in oak barrels that hold no more than 200 litres.

Pechuga Pioneered by producer Del Maguey, this style is distilled a third time for twenty-four hours in the presence of fruit, nuts, a little uncooked rice and a washed chicken breast that's suspended inside the still. The addition of the chicken breast is claimed to diminish the otherwise dominating fruity character of this style of mezcal.

MEZCAL PRODUCTION

Generally, producers operate on a small scale and handcraft their products. Traditionally, the *piñas* are not steamed as happens with tequila, but slow roasted on hot stones in pits that are covered with earth or waste from the plant to prevent the *piñas* from catching fire. This guarantees that the *piñas* absorb the earthy, pungent smokiness that is so distinctive in mezcal. About three days later, the *piñas* are crushed and mashed.

The entire contents of the vat are then transferred to a pot still, traditionally for a single but, more usually, for double distillation. Column stills are also used. Mezcal can reach an alcoholic content of 55% ABV and the distillate may be left to age in barrels as indicated by the age classifications above.

Roasting pit

PULQUE

A potent drink that was enjoyed long before the days of the Columbians, pulque was reserved for the pleasure of the privileged few, as well as to render senseless those destined for religious sacrifice. Rich in vitamins and nutrients, it was also given to the elderly and pregnant women in the Aztec culture. Still consumed today, though declining in popularity, its sour-sweet character and surprising kick tend to be an acquired taste.

AGAVE NECTAR

This sweet syrup is produced from the heart of any agave plant. It is a highly nutritious, natural sweetener that rates low on the glycaemic index and so has been marketed as being an ideal sugar substitute for diabetics. The *piñas* are heated only enough to release their sap before they are chopped and passed through a centrifuge to separate the syrup from the solids. The resulting syrup is thinner than honey and sweeter than sugar.

Quiz on tequila and mezcal

1. Tequila that is classified as 'regular' uses sugars from what raw materials?

    A. Blue agave only
    B. Agave only
    C. Agave and non-agave sugars
    D. Blue agave and non-agave sugars

2. In what year did tequila gain global recognition as a product exclusive to Mexico?

    A. 1954
    B. 1964
    C. 1974
    D. 1984

3. Tequila can only be distilled in how many demarcated areas?

    A. One
    B. Five
    C. Three
    D. Seven

4. In regular tequila what is the minimum percentage of sugars that must come from the blue agave?

    A. 45%
    B. 49%
    C. 51%
    D. 55%

5. The bigger and sweeter agave plants grow in which area in Mexico?

    A. Highlands
    B. Lowlands
    C. Tequila valley
    D. Tequila town

6. In what year was José Maria Guadalupe de Cuervo granted the first commercial licence to produce 'agave wine'?

   A 1695
   B. 1725
   C. 1765
   D. 1795

7. The blue agave is also called the 'century plant' because of the long time the plant takes to flower. Generally, how long does it take?

   A. 4–6 years
   B. 5–9 years
   C. 7–12 years
   D. 10–15 years

8. Which of these terms can be applied to unaged tequila?

   A. Blanco
   B. Plata
   C. Silver
   D. All of these

9. Which state in Mexico produces around 99% of all tequila?

   A. Jalisco
   B. Nayarit
   C. Tamaulipas
   D. Guanajuato

10. Tequila classified as *reposado* must be rested (aged) for a minimum of how many months?

    A. One month
    B. Two months
    C. Four months
    D. Eight months

11. Tequila classified as *añejo* must be aged for a minimum of how many months?

   A. 12 months
   B. 15 months
   C. 24 months
   D. 36 months

12. What is the name given to the skilled workers who harvest the agave plants?

   A. *Quiotes*
   B. *Agaveros*
   C. *Piñas*
   D. *Jimadors*

13. What is the name given to the traditional oven used to cook the agaves?

   A. Autoclave
   B. *Tahona*
   C. *Horno*
   D. *Penca*

14. What is the name given to the sugary sap that's crushed or washed out from the cooked agave plants?

   A. *Ordinario*
   B. *Aqua miel*
   C. Tequila
   D. *Mosto*

15. In tequila production what is the name given to the distillate retained from the first distillation?

   A. *Ordinario*
   B. *Aqua miel*
   C. Tequila
   D. *Mosto*

16. When a spirit is to be commercialized as tequila the alcohol strength off the still must lie between what levels?

A. 30%–45% ABV
B. 35%–55% ABV
C. 40%–60% ABV
D. No restrictions

17. What is the meaning of the phrase *con gusano* on a label of mezcal?

A. Contains a worm
B. Contains flavourings
C. Contains the larva of a moth
D. Contains added sugars

18. What cooking process is used to generate mezcal's distinctive smokiness?

A. Roasting
B. Steaming
C. Boiling
D. Pressure cooking

19. To be called *añejo* the tequila must have been aged in oak barrels with a capacity no greater than what?

A. 200 litres
B. 400 litres
C. 600 litres
D. 750 litres

20. The agave plant used to make tequila is classified as a member of what plant family?

A. Cactus
B. Penca
C. Yucca
D. Lily

21. In the production of tequila, *mosto muerto* is the name given to the liquid created by what process?

    A. Crushing
    B. Cooking
    C. Fermentation
    D. Distillation

MAKING COCKTAILS WITH TEQUILA

Tequila is the most divisive of spirit categories, with cries of 'Never again,' from swathes of the audience, probably the ones who over-indulged in cheap, poor quality shots in their youth, whenever it is mentioned. Conversely it is the base spirit for the world's most popular cocktail, the Margarita. Distinctive styles from highland and lowland distilleries coupled with over nine-hundred different brands and bottlings mean tequila requires time to learn to mix it to the best effect – and that is before you consider the rapidly expanding availability of similar spirits from Mexico, such as mezcal, bacanora, raicilla and sotol.

Two factors contribute to the intricacies of mixing with agave spirits. Firstly the low distillation proof, compounded by the preferred use of quite short-necked and simple stills, results in lots of complex flavour molecules, rooted in the raw agave, remaining in the final spirit. The second is the climate where ageing occurs. Huge changes between day and night time temperatures drive continual ingress and egress of spirit into and out of the barrel. This combines with a low relative humidity to age the agave spirit faster than any other spirit category and this, in turn, changes the nature of flavours drawn from the second- and third-fill barrels. These factors mean that it is usual to consider only the younger styles of blanco and reposado as candidates for cocktails, with anejos and extra anejos, best enjoyed neat.

The Margarita

Being the world's most popular cocktail, variations are to be expected regarding how the drink is made and presented to match differing tastes of consumers around the globe. The major division is between the Margaritas blended with ice and served frozen and the more traditional shaken drinks, served straight up.

Frozen Margaritas are delicious, and perfect for a hot day, but the addition of so much water from the blending process means that extra sugar must be added to counteract the dilution and maintain balance. The quest for this balance causes much of the discussion around the perfect recipe for the shaken version. A simple Tequila Sour or a Tommy's Margarita, using agave syrup, calls for a roughly even balance between sweet and sour, but the classic recipe uses Cointreau as the sweet ingredient. This causes difficulty setting the ratio of ingredients because Cointreau is considerably less sweet than simple or agave syrup and so a larger quantity is required to balance a given amount of lime juice. Increasing the amount of Cointreau however also increases significantly the quantity of alcohol, as Cointreau is 40% abv (eighty proof). Therefore creating the perfect Margarita is something of a balancing act, requiring finesse in measurement. Assuredly though it is worth the effort.

45ml blanco tequila
22.5ml Cointreau
20ml lime juice

Margaritas are normally served in a glass rimmed with salt. This is often done by dipping the rim of the glass first in lime juice and next into a tray of salt. Do not do this. Instead, carefully moisten the required area of the glass with lime juice; it is often a good idea only to rim half the glass to allow the consumer the choice. Lightly dust the *outside* of the glass only with salt and wipe away any excess, taking extra care to ensure no salt goes into the glass.

Place the liquid ingredients into a cocktail shaker and shake with ice. Strain into the salt-rimmed glass (this is one of the few occasions where the glass should not be chilled as condensation will cause the salt to melt and make the stem of the glass sticky). Garnish with a lime wedge or wheel on the rim of the glass delineating the salted side if this method is chosen.

Margaritas can be made with highland or lowland tequilas as the drink works well with both the full bodied and lighter styles but try using a blanco tequila if possible. The clean flavours of lime and orange do not benefit from being clouded with the flavours of aging. With reposado Margaritas some of the purity of expression is lost.

El Diablo

Tequila has the strength of character to stand up to powerful ingredients; the Diablo is one such pairing. Originally made with ginger ale, this drink is massively improved with the substitution of spicy ginger beer. There are lots of good quality brands available but look for one that is bottle fermented as they have the most complex (and fiery) flavour. The Diablo is sweetened with crème de cassis, which sinks when added, producing a graduated fade similar in appearance to the far inferior in taste Tequila Sunrise.

50ml reposado tequila
juice of half a lime
170ml spicy ginger beer
10ml crème de cassis

In a large highball glass add the tequila and fresh lime; this is best squeezed straight into the glass. If you can find one in your kitchen equipment retailer a Mexican arm press is the perfect tool for squeezing limes for drinks and cooking and is a great addition to your cocktail kit. Top up with ginger beer and stir. Gently drizzle the cassis over the top of the drink; it should slowly settle leaving a delicate pink to purple graduation. Garnish with a lime wedge.

If you like spicy food or love ginger it is worth making your own sparkling ginger. Peel fresh ginger and put through a centrifugal juicer. Add the resultant very spicy juice to an equal weight of sugar and mix until dissolved. This syrup can then be spritzed with soda water to make a healthy and delicious fresh ginger beer.

Due to the strength of ginger beer this drink works best with a lowland reposado tequila with a full body. If you fancy using a lighter style or a blanco tequila try using ginger ale instead.

Honeydew Margarita

There are many variations on the theme of the Margarita; one of the very finest is this version using melon. Tequila works well with watermelon and cantaloupe but the natural affinity between tequila and honey – the juice of the cooked agave is called agua miel meaning honey water – makes the honeydew melon the perfect match.

50ml reposado tequila
10ml honey syrup
10ml agave syrup
20ml lime juice
50g honeydew melon

Honey is both a healthy and delicious cocktail ingredient but care must be taken in its use. When it gets cold even the runniest honey will solidify and, when shaken, the honey will not amalgamate with the other ingredients. This can be rectified by cutting the honey with water before use. Add one part of hot water to three parts of honey and stir vigorously until homogenized. This syrup can be kept refrigerated for up to two weeks.

Crush the melon thoroughly with a pestle or cocktail muddler in a cocktail shaker and add the other ingredients. Shake hard and strain into a chilled cocktail glass. Serve with a thin slice of melon dusted with Tajin, a traditional fruit seasoning. If this is unavailable it is easy to make at home for a perfect accompaniment to fruits and it is amazing on corn on the cob. Simply soak chopped chillies in fresh lime juice for a couple of hours and dry in an oven at 75°C (170°F) until crisp. Blend in a processor and mix two parts of the dried ground chilli with one of coarse sea salt. This will keep for six months in the larder.

Try this drink with a reposado tequila from the highlands; the floral notes of the agave work well with the fragrant melon and the honey syrup pairs well with the vanilla and oak notes from the barrel aging.

6

GENEVER AND GIN

THE ORIGINS OF GENEVER (JENEVER)

The word 'genever' comes from the French word for the juniper berry, *genièvre*. The medicinal use of juniper berries was recorded as long ago as 1500BC, in an Egyptian cure for tapeworm. In 1269, in Damme, near Bruges, Jacob van Maerlant, one of the Middle Ages' most renowned authors, wrote about the medical benefits of cooking juniper berries in wine. In the middle of the fourteenth century the smoke from burning juniper was used as protection against the Black Death, a disease which killed almost half Europe's population. The medieval herbalist Culpepper also recommended juniper for treating flatulence.

There is evidence of large-scale distillation in Bruges in the thirteenth and fifteenth centuries. When most of what is now known as Belgium and the Netherlands was one country under the rule of Spain the peoples of this area were among Europe's most renowned distillers. Those that fled the Spanish occupation in the seventeenth century and settled in the northern provinces (the Netherlands) became known as the Dutch.

The Dutch became great explorers and the exotic herbs, fruits and spices their navy brought back to Amsterdam were welcomed by the distillers who combined them with local botanicals, like juniper and caraway, to help mask some of the less palatable characteristics of their raw spirit and to transform some distillates into medicines which, in turn, they offered to sailors as protection against disease.

There is no evidence of the Dutch inventing juniper flavoured alcohols and neither is it likely that Professor Franciscus Sylvius of Leiden University was the 'father' of genever, as he was born in 1614, by which time genever was already in production. In fact genever evolved over the centuries, most likely in the cities of first Belgium and then Holland, where, in 1572, another Leiden University professor and chemist, Sylvius de Bouve, is credited with being the first to blend juniper oil with unaged grain alcohol, as opposed to water or wine and prescribing this genever as an inexpensive diuretic and cure for stomach upsets, bladder infections and kidney stones.

The word genever first appeared in a Dutch dictionary in 1672 and by the second half of that century Bols, Nolet, De Kuyper and hundreds of others were distilling in the town of Schiedam. By the eighteenth century this town, now absorbed into the Rotterdam region, had become the biggest genever city, centered upon the port's importation of grain. In 1882 the town boasted forty malt houses, ten glass factories and twenty-two windmills to support the distillers of genever, or what was also called 'Hollands' or 'Schiedam'. (At the time Amsterdam was the centre of the sugar and spice trade and so focused on liqueur production.)

By 1820, genever had replaced beer as the national drink in the Low Countries and later in that century genever outsold London gin in America by 6:1. James Edward Alexander's 1833 book *Transatlantic Sketches* includes the exchange: ' "Have you got any good gin, sir?" "Yes, sir, Hollands." "Well, mix me a cocktail, I want to wet up." '

Genever, not gin, was a recognized cocktail spirit alongside whisky, rum and brandy. In his 1862 cocktail book, Jerry Thomas specifies genever or Hollands in more recipes than gin. Only circumstances such as Prohibition, the increasing popularity of dry vermouth and the Dry Martini, as well as a failure to produce genever during two world wars caused sales of genever to decline during the twentieth century. However, the twenty-first century may witness its revival as more people discover genever to be the blank spot on the mixologist's canvas between gin and scotch.

HOW DOES GENEVER DIFFER FROM GIN?

For genever, a whisky-like mash of malted barley, rye, wheat and corn is fermented for as long as five days to produce the malty core or so-called 'malt wine' at around 10% ABV. This is distilled three times or more but only to low levels of alcohol in order to retain some of the grain character that is key to the distinctive nature of genever. Some of this malt distillate may then be redistilled with flavourings or blended with neutral spirit.

Genever must include juniper distillate, though this need not be a dominant characteristic or even perceptible. Other flavourings include the likes of cloves, coriander, ginger, angelica, aniseed and caraway. The flavourings need not be distillates. Instead, they may be the result of maceration and/or percolation. Each recipe uses the botanicals in different ratios.

Though traditional genever would have been 100% malt, today most styles require some of this malt spirit to be blended, in varying proportions, with neutral spirit distilled from grain or sugar beet.

STYLES OF GENEVER

Jonge A neutral spirit distilled in a continuous still, although some distillers then refine the spirit in a pot still. However, distillate that is bottled as jonge genever is still heavier than the spirit found in a bottle of London Dry gin or in a bottle of vodka because malt spirit has been added to a maximum level of 15%. The minimum ABV is 35% and a maximum addition of ten grams of sugar per litre is permitted.

Oude This refers to the traditional style of genever and not to its age. It must contain a minimum of 15% malt spirit, though in Belgium, the percentage is likely to be greater. The minimum ABV is 35% but the actual ABV is usually 38% and a maximum of twenty grams of sugar per litre may be added. Any straw colour may result either from wood maturation or from the addition of caramel. Ageing of genever is not obligatory but, if chosen, maturation must be in oak casks, with a capacity no larger then 700 litres, for at least one year, and the years must be stated on the label.

Korenwijn Must contain a minimum of 51% malt spirit and no more than a maximum of twenty grams of sugar per litre may be added. It is often aged and usually for more than the minimum of one year. In fact, two and a half years is more usual with the early months possibly in relatively new wood.

Graanjenever Is distilled 100% from grain. The minimum bottling strength is 35% ABV.

GIN: A TALE OF RAGS TO RICHES

Gin was described by Lord Kinross, in his book *The Kindred Spirit*, as the ardent spirit which rose from the gutter to become the respected companion of civilized man. This was an accurate description of gin's journey from the slums of eighteenth-century London, through improvements in quality in the nineteenth century, to its status today as a truly international spirit.

With English troops supporting the Dutch in their revolt against Spain in 1585 and thousands of Dutch trading there in the seventeenth century, some knowledge of genever must have already existed in London. However from 1618 to 1648, fighting alongside the Dutch against the Spanish, the English witnessed the Dutch soldiers knocking back shots of genever before going into battle. They described this habit as taking 'Dutch courage', a phrase that remains in use today.

At this time, the Scots and Irish drank whisky while the English consumed beer if they were poor or wine and cognac if wealthy. But in the 1660s, the diarist Samuel Pepys was writing, in London, of a strong water made with juniper. When soldiers returned with their taste for genever, the seeds of gin drinking were sown in ports like Plymouth and London. In 1689, the Dutch protestant William of Orange replaced James II as King of England and declared war on Catholic France. Steps were taken to reduce French imports and, to this end, William encouraged the production of local spirits using grain, a first for England.

'Gin Lane' by Hogarth

Called upon to be patriotic and drink for England, the masses responded enthusiastically. The popularity of gin, the English corruption of the word genever, grew as an escape from disease and degradation. But unfortunately, for all too many, an early death was the only real escape. One sign outside a Southwark inn famously read: 'Drunk for a 1d. Dead drunk for 2d. Clean straw for nothing.'

By 1750, gin had become the choice of the masses and a source of widespread drunkenness and death because of the lethal ingredients in many of the concoctions. Hogarth sketched vivid records of the drunkenness and misery. At this time the most popular gin was sweetened, heavily flavoured with juniper and called 'Old Tom'.

Only the arrival of the continuous still in the 1830s permitted many of the harmful impurities to be removed along with the sugar and glycerine. More subtle and exotic flavourings were used to enhance rather than to mask the raw spirit. Gin's reputation improved with the emergence of a drier 'London' style of gin.

GIN AND THE ROYAL NAVY

Initially, flavourings were introduced into this cleaner and drier spirit as much for their medicinal value as for their taste. The Royal Navy was quick to recognize gin's potential benefits as protection against disease when sailing the tropics. But still, gin remained relatively unpalatable, at least until the Royal Navy discovered the benefits of lemons. This unfamiliar exotic fruit, originally from the east, not only helped to prevent scurvy but, better still, it improved the taste of gin. For similar reasons, in the nineteenth century, the Royal Navy also adopted Pink Gin.

A German doctor, in the town of Angostura in Venezuela, had perfected a blend of bitters containing bark from the Angostura tree. Sailors added drops of this Angostura to their gin to enjoy the bitters' medicinal benefit as a cure for stomach ailments. But, again, they found that the addition helped to improve the gin's taste.

Quinine was another essential part of the sailors' fight for health. It tasted awful but was key in their battle against malaria. Born in 1740, Jacob Schweppe was an amateur scientist who perfected the process of making mineral soda water. He moved his business from Switzerland to Covent Garden in London, where he met with great success, retiring in 1798. By the second half of the nineteenth century, subsequent owners of the Schweppes company developed and patented a soda water with added quinine which they commercialized as Indian Tonic Water and shipped to the grateful Services. Gin and tonic with a slice of lemon became the beverage of choice throughout the colonies in the East.

Returning home, servicemen continued to enjoy their Pink Gins and gin and tonics with a slice of lemon. This encouraged many distillers to start gin businesses during the Victorian era. Gin's reputation improved and distillers introduced different recipes for the drier styles of gin, many of which remain well known today.

The gin pennant, a small green triangular flag, sporting a wine glass, continues to give evidence of gin's popularity amongst Royal Navy officers. When raised, it signifies a ship's wardroom is issuing an invitation to officers from other ships to board for cocktails.

Gin pennant

By the twentieth century, London gin had acquired recognition as a world-class, quality spirit, particularly in America. There, gin was a popular choice during Prohibition even though many bottlings consisted of cheap alcohol mixed with various flavourings and glycerine. Even homemade 'bathtub gin', all too often a lethal mixture of industrial alcohol, glycerine and oil of juniper carried some romance. Contrary to popular belief, bathtub gin was not made in a bathtub. Rather, the preferred bottles were too tall to be filled with water from a sink, so they were filled from a bathtub tap. Many cocktails were probably created to mask the awful taste of these so-called gins. After Prohibition it was London Dry, rather than genever, that remained popular.

As the belief grew that drinking should be valued as a civilized pursuit, gin became recognized, more than any other spirit, as the choice of sophisticates, a truly international spirit, classless and enjoyed equally by both sexes.

HOW GIN IS MADE

Gin is an agricultural product, not an industrial creation. There are three methods of production but in all cases the base liquid is pure neutral spirit, distilled to 96% ABV. If this base spirit is to be redistilled, it will be reduced in strength to about 45% ABV with pure water before the distiller adds the chosen botanicals. Recipes remain unique to each distiller but, according to regulations, the predominant flavour must be juniper.

To best extract the essential oils from the botanicals distillation is executed in a traditional pot still. If, during distillation, the cut is made early in the process, the gin will tend to be light with good citric character. If the cut is made late, the gin will tend to be fuller-bodied and more rooty.

EUROPEAN UNION DEFINITIONS

Gin Is a neutral spirit, simply cold compounded with natural flavourings or artificial essences. Sweetening and colouring are also permitted. Such gin cannot be called London or carry the description 'distilled'.

Distilled gin Must result from a diluted, neutral spirit that has been redistilled in the presence of natural botanicals, such as juniper, coriander and citrus peel. Colouring is permitted and flavourings may be added after the distillation. When the neutral spirit and botanicals are heated, the alcohols vaporize and rise as steam, carrying the flavour compounds. These vapours then cool and condense into a more concentrated and flavoured distillate. This process tends to generate rich botanical attachments.

London distilled gin Is a style of distilled gin. All flavourings must be natural and present during the redistillation of the neutral spirit. No flavourings may be added after distillation and no colouring is permitted. The word 'dry' may be added to the label. 'London' is not a geographical definition but a description of a gin produced in accordance with these regulations.

Prior to the distillation of both distilled and London gins the botanicals may first be steeped in spirit to encourage more attachment between the alcohol and the botanicals. This process is costly but tends to yield more complexity and depth of flavour and causes the gin to retain its flavour longer, once poured into a glass.

Some distillers use a Carter Head still, in which the botanicals are placed in a perforated copper box or basket, situated in the neck above the spirit. Only the spirit vapours are able to come into contact with the botanicals in this process, known as 'racking' or 'flavour infusion'. This is ideal for the attachment of delicate flavours that might otherwise be damaged by direct contact with the spirit and so tends to be used to produce the more delicate styles of gin.

Distilled gins are able to retain more of the subtle, complex and long lasting flavours than cold compounded gins. Maturation is not required as the spirit has been highly rectified during distillation to remove the fusel oils and other impurities. If stored for too long gin can even deteriorate and lose its freshness but there are examples of gins that have been aged for specific individuality.

Bottling strength The minimum bottling strength is 37.5% ABV but the alcohol strength does play an important role in taste delivery. Alcohol not only delivers a pleasant warming sensation but it also binds the flavours that have been distilled into the gin. Just as there is an optimum temperature for the serving of wines so there are strengths at which certain botanicals are best fixed in a gin. At low levels of alcohol some character will not be captured at all whereas when high strength gins are diluted in the glass, at a ratio of around 3:1, the aromatic release from the botanicals can be much more complex and rewarding.

SOME OF THE MORE POPULAR GIN BOTANICALS

The Dutch and English dominated the exotic fruit and spice trade and the fruits, spices and herbs they discovered while trading around the globe became key to the creation and development of both genever and gin. It is the individuality and character of these botanicals that combine to create the different gins or 'liquid steel', a very apt American phrase for the taste impact of a great gin. The number of different botanicals used by each distiller varies from just a few to very many, but quality should always be judged on how the flavourings interact and the overall balance and complexity achieved rather than on the quantity of flavourings.

- **Almond** Bitter almonds are ground to release their oils.

- **Angelica** An aromatic and earthy root with floral character, used to fix other flavours in the spirit.

- **Cardamom** Seeds from a member of the ginger family used to sweeten the breath and aid digestion.

- **Cassia bark** A relative of cinnamon, but stronger and more bitter with a smell and taste of chewing gum.

- **Coriander** The second most commonly used botanical, similar to parsley but with citrus undertones.

- **Citrus peel** A clean, tart flavour that can be either sweet or dry and rich in the oils used to enhance gin's refreshing qualities.

- **Cubeb berries** A member of the pepper family, from Java, that has spicy, peppery aromas.

- **Grains of paradise** An intensely peppery berry, often used to enhance contributions of other botanicals.

- **Juniper berries** A bittersweet, purple berry, native to Europe, used to generate gin's core flavour and essential freshness with hints of pine, lavender and camphor.

- **Liquorice** A bittersweet root.

- **Nutmeg** Brings warm, sweet, musky flavours and aromas to the gin.

- **Orris root** The root of the Florentine iris, used to help fix the flavours in the spirit.

OTHER GIN STYLES

Plymouth A richer, oilier and fruitier style of gin that conforms with the definition of London distilled gin but which, in style, lies somewhere between London distilled gin and genever and which must be made in Plymouth, in the Black Friars Distillery, according to EU Geographical Designation.

Old Tom A style of gin popular in eighteenth- and nineteenth-century England that was sweetened to mask the rough nature of the spirit distilled in pots before the arrival of continuous distillation. This was very much the choice of the poor for whom the sugar would have represented useful calories in what, otherwise, were inadequate diets. The style is now available as a speciality gin.

Steinhäger A German gin that is distilled using only juniper berries as flavouring.

Mahon or Xorigeur Like Plymouth gin, this is a gin style that can be distilled only in one place, Mahon, the capital of Menorca, according to EU law. This gin was first distilled when the Royal Navy captured the deep-water harbour on this Spanish island and retained it as their Mediterranean base. The gin is made from wine alcohol with botanicals suspended over the boiling liquid so that only the vapours pass through it.

Quiz on gin and genever

1. The word 'genever' is derived from a French word meaning what?

   A. Geneva
   B. Juniper
   C. Gin
   D. Gender

2. Who is credited with being the first to blend juniper oil with grain spirit?

   A. Franciscus Sylvius
   B. Sylvius de Bouve
   C. Lucas Bols
   D. Petrus De Kuyper

3. Which Dutch town was the historical centre for the production of genever?

   A. Schiedam
   B. Amsterdam
   C. Rotterdam
   D. Utrecht

4. The quantity of malt spirit in a jonge genever must not exceed what percentage?

   A. 5%
   B. 10%
   C. 15%
   D. 20%

5. What does the term *oude* mean when applied to genever?

   A. Aged in barrel
   B. Caramel added
   C. Old bottling
   D. Traditional style

6. The quantity of malt spirit in korenwijn must account for no less than what percentage?

   A. 15%
   B. 49%
   C. 51%
   D. 75%

7. By what date had gin become the choice of the London masses?

A. 1600
B. 1650
C. 1700
D. 1750

8. According to EU regulations which botanical must provide gin's predominant flavour?

A. Juniper berry
B. Angelica
C. Coriander
D. Orris root

9. Which style of gin requires all botanicals to be present during redistillation of the neutral spirit?

A. Gin
B. Compounded gin
C. Distilled gin
D. London distilled gin

10. Which of these stills would be the choice of a distiller wanting to use delicate botanicals?

A. Pot still
B. Column still
C. Carter Head still
D. Copper still

11. London Dry distilled gin can only be made where?

A. Anywhere in the world
B. Any town in England
C. Plymouth
D. London

12. What is the name of a style of sweetened gin, popular in eighteenth- and nineteenth-century London?

    A. Mahon
    B. Old Tom
    C. Black Friars
    D. Old Samuels

13. Ageing of oude genever is not obligatory but, if chosen, what is the maximum permitted capacity of the barrel used?

    A. 250 litres
    B. 400 litres
    C. 700 litres
    D. 750 litres

14. In the latter half of the nineteenth century genever outsold gin in the USA by what ratio?

    A. 2:1
    B. 4.1
    C. 6:1
    D. 8:1

15. Drinking genever in the Netherlands prompted which of these phrases still used in the English language?

    A. Dutch courage
    B. Going Dutch
    C. Double Dutch
    D. Dutch metal

16. Which King of England encouraged early distillation of the spirit that was to become known as gin?

    A. James I
    B. William of Orange
    C. Henry V
    D. Richard III

17. Which botanical was introduced into gin to provide protection against scurvy?

    A. Quinine
    B. Orris root
    C. Citrus peel
    D. Cassia bark

18. Which are the three most common botanicals used in the distillation of gin?

    A. Juniper, orris & citrus peel
    B. Juniper, angelica & citrus peel
    C. Juniper, coriander & licorice
    D. Juniper, coriander & angelica

19. Which of these gins enjoy(s) EU Geographical Designation?

    A. Plymouth only
    B. Plymouth and London
    C. Plymouth, Steinhäger and Mahon
    D. Plymouth and Mahon

20. What process is used by some distillers to encourage more attachment between botanicals and alcohol?

    A. Heating
    B. Steeping
    C. Extraction
    D. Pot distillation

1. B; 2. B; 3. A; 4. C; 5. D; 6. C; 7. D; 8. A; 9. D; 10. C; 11. A; 12. B; 13. C; 14. C; 15. A; 16. B; 17. C; 18. C; 19. D; 20. B

Answers

MAKING COCKTAILS WITH GIN

Gin is the foundation of the majority of drinks from the golden age of cocktails and has found favour with modern mixologists for the same reasons. It is adaptable, working in short and long drinks, pairs well with other spirits and vermouths as well as fruit and other fresh ingredients and its aroma brings an extra dimension to almost any mixed drink.

The Dry Martini

'The only American invention as perfect as a sonnet' – H.L.Mencken

As with many important inventions there are still arguments as to the genesis of the Dry Martini. As with the light bulb, radio and penicillin, the inventors responded to both new technology and an unfilled niche. This opportunity for parallel evolution means that, once the ingredients of this most simple of drinks had become available, the drink was probably 'invented' many times.

The reason this drink has transcended its basic ingredients to become the visual representation of the cocktail on neon signs around the world is down to the almost infinite number of variations. Humanity craves individuality and personalization, and bartenders have always benefitted from making a drink for a customer 'just so'.

For the intrepid explorer in the world of spirits and cocktails this process of creating the perfect Martini is one of experimentation. Each combination of a different gin and vermouth provides a new taste experience. Once favourites are chosen the ratio of the ingredients brings out nuance and variation and the use of a savoury garnish can provide the perfect link from the aperitif to the dining table.

Because of the number of variations it is almost impossible to write a recipe for a Gin Martini but there are some guidelines worth following. A Martini should be served bitingly cold. It is therefore advisable to keep ingredients, including garnish, in the fridge and glassware in the freezer until the last possible moment. Gin can vary quite widely in abv and in cocktail circles there is still some discussion as to whether the more alcoholic gins should be stirred longer to lower their alcohol level to one consistent with a standard proof gin or to stir in a manner to deliver a level of dilution that maintains the variation in alcoholic strength. This type of nuance in methodology is why making this drink can be so rewarding but, in all cases, one of the most important decisions is how big to make the drink. It is often a good idea to match the number of sips to the number of garnishes but most cocktail glasses are too large for this, negatively affecting both the length of an enjoyable evening and the drinker's liver. If in doubt stick to a maximum of 60ml of spirit.

The author's Martini

60ml London dry gin
5ml French vermouth
1 large twist of lemon peel
3 pimento stuffed olives

In a large mixing glass stir the ingredients with 250g ice straight from the freezer until the cubes just become suspended in the liquid. Strain into a chilled cocktail glass and garnish with the spray from a large lemon twist, which can be discarded, and three olives. When in doubt serve more olives on the side.

The Dry Martini tastes wonderful with all styles of gin, so practice with what you have at hand or explore the shelves of the liquor store with confidence. Changing the ratio of gin to vermouth will allow you to balance the flavour of different styles.

Tom Collins

Gin's most common bedfellow is of course tonic water, a happy case of two medicinal ingredients complementing each other, or in actuality, the inebriating effects of gin making the historically vital consumption of the antimalarial quinine more palatable. (Modern tonic water bears no relation to the original stuff, containing less than 1% of the amount of profoundly bitter cinchona extract key to an effective medicine.)

Even now the T of G and T is an acquired taste, the acquisition of which might have been better off spent enjoying a Tom Collins. No other way of consumption, short of neat gin, allows for a better comparison of brands and styles of gin, while providing the perfect refreshing highball.

At its most simple a Tom Collins is just gin and homemade sparkling lemonade. Indeed it is very easy to serve, for large groups, in the mode of a pitcher of old fashioned lemonade. The key to a great Tom Collins is the balance between sweet and sour and this injects into the drink's creation the only possible difficulty because individuals have different appreciations of what the perfect balance might be. Some people enjoy eating lemons straight from the tree; others put maple syrup on bacon.

To make a basic lemonade it is easier to use a simple syrup that has been made in advance, instead of powdered sugar. Simply mix equal parts by weight of caster or superfine sugar and water and allow the sugar to dissolve. Once completely dissolved this can then be used for all sweet and sour drinks. The benefit of using this simple syrup instead of a thicker, proprietary or cooked syrup is that it produces a pleasing balance for most when used in equal parts with lemon juice. If in doubt err slightly on the sweet side and serve with a citrus wedge, allowing the drinker to adjust the balance slightly by squeezing the garnish into the drink

The nature of this drink means that it will obviously work with citrusy gins but the amount of dilution can mean that a bold juniper-led brand will work even better.

50ml gin
25ml freshly squeezed lemon juice
25ml simple syrup
75ml soda water

Pour all ingredients over ice into a large highball glass and garnish with a lemon wedge and a cherry.

As well as being a great way to assess the character of different gins in a cocktail, the Tom Collins is a great base for adaptations. Try muddling fresh fruits or herbs before mixing. Add a dash of liqueur or fruit syrup, or even experiment with flavoured sodas. It is also a great place to try more historical styles of gin, with sweetened 'Old Tom' gins requiring small reductions in the amount of simple syrup. For the adventurous the Tom Collins is also an excellent way of mixing with genever, softening but not overpowering genever's malt character.

Space Gin Smash

A smash, as its name implies, is a style of cocktail where fruits are first muddled and then shaken and served over cracked or crushed ice. This process brings out more flavour than shaking alone or using juices, particularly with lemons or limes, where significant quantities of aromatic and slightly bitter oils are then incorporated into the drink.

The Space Gin Smash was created in 2004 by Pete Kendall and is one of the very best versions of this style of drink. Muddled red grapes provide natural sweetness and the floral notes from the mint and elderflower complement the herbaceous character of the gin.

50ml London dry gin
3 lemon wedges
5 red grapes
15ml elderflower cordial
6 mint leaves
50ml pressed apple juice

Muddle fruit in a cocktail shaker and add the other ingredients. Shake with ice and strain over crushed ice into a 12oz rocks glass. Garnish with a lemon wedge, apple slice and sprig of mint.

This drink works well with any style of gin but the floral nature of the ingredients means that it is a perfect drink to make with a lighter citrusy, peppery gin that might get lost in a cocktail with more strident ingredients.

7

OTHER FLAVOURED WHITE SPIRITS

ABSINTHE

There is a long history of medicinal use of wormwood. Medicines using wormwood leaves combined with alcohol are recorded in Egyptian texts as early as 1550BC. Wormwood is mentioned in the Bible, in the Book of Genesis, as a remedy for plague and cholera. Wormwood flavoured wines were recorded by Hippocrates in Greece as a cure for digestive disorders and flatulence and to rid the body of tapeworms. Pliny the Elder rewarded Roman chariot champions with wines steeped with bittersweet wormwood.

Modern references to absinthe-like drinks can be found in the Neuchâtel region of Switzerland from the 1750s. These became widespread between 1789 and 1799, when French loyalists took refuge from the French Revolution in Switzerland and its neighbouring countries. One of those exiles, Dr. Pierre Ordinaire supposedly created, but more likely bought and sold, recipes for such drinks as tonics. By 1797, one of those recipes, allegedly made by the two Henriot sisters in Couvet, was bought by a Major Dubied to produce and market himself. With his son and son-in-law, M Perrenoud another émigré, he opened his distillery in Couvet, Switzerland. Perrenoud then changed his name to Pernod. To cope with increased demand and to avoid import taxes, Pernod Fils was established in 1805 across the border, in Pontarlier, France;

this was the country's first commercial distillery of an anise-based spirit.

Sales in France grew and many imitations appeared as this wine-based spirit, flavoured with Artemisia absinthium (wormwood), green aniseed, fennel and hyssop became more and more popular. In the 1840s, during the Algerian War, the French Foreign Legion took a daily absinthe ration to fight malaria. Troops brought their habit back to the Paris cafés. By the 1850s absinthe was a favourite drink of, and inspiration for, painters like Manet and Degas.

Artemisia absinthium

Initially, the spirit was wine based but the phylloxera blight's destruction of so many vines in the late nineteenth century (see Cognac chapter) forced distillers to turn to grain. The popularity of absinthe soared because one glass was just a tenth of the price of a bottle of wine and a third of the price of a loaf of bread. Five in the afternoon became known as *l'heure verte* (the green hour) and towards the end of the 1800s, conservative France was denouncing absinthe as the choice of decadents and the opiate of Bohemian youth, the cause of their outrageous lifestyle, their hallucinations and mental health problems. Many Parisians would ask for *une correspondence*, meaning a ticket to the lunatic asylum, when ordering an absinthe.

'The Absinthe Drinker' by Victor Oliva

Genuine concerns focused on thujone, the essential oil of wormwood and a compound similar to an active component of marijuana. The hypothesis was that the two could affect the brain in similar ways. But the truth is that the leaves of the plant are fairly innocuous. In fact, sage contains more thujone than wormwood. And none of the original, nor the modern, absinthe brands contain any more than trace elements of this chemical. Today, in alcoholic drinks prepared with any *Artemisia* species, the EU permits thujone levels of no more than thirty-five parts per million and the USA, no more than ten.

No doubt helped by a campaign that was funded by wine growers to denigrate absinthe and undermine its overwhelming popularity, the spirit was banned in Belgium in 1905 and in Holland in 1908. By the early twentieth century 'absinthism' was declared a disease. A dreadful triple murder, committed by a farm labourer who had drunk seven glasses of wine, seven glasses of cognac, two coffees laced with brandy, two crèmes de menthe and two absinthes resulted in the spirit being banned in Switzerland in 1910. Drinks with more than ten parts per million of thujone were banned in America in 1912. There, it was replaced in 1935 with Herbsaint, which is still America's only home-produced anise liqueur. Sales were banned in

France in 1914 and, in 1915, the ban was made formal. Small-scale production continued in Spain and Portugal. Sales were never formally banned in the UK. Supplies just dried up.

With common sense most people would have realized that the threats to human health were more likely posed by absinthe's strength, up to 75% ABV, rather than by the thujone level and that the mental health problems of many resulted from chronic syphilis rather than from absinthe.

In 1920 sales of aniseed drinks were sanctioned once more, but the use of wormwood remained illegal. The spirit's modern revival dates back to the collapse of the Iron Curtain and to Czech entrepreneur Radomil Hill who, in 1989, started to produce absinth (without an 'e' in Czech).

Following relaxation of the legislation in France, an Englishman, George Rowley, secured the UK government's authorization for the legal sale of absinthe in the European Union and worked closely with Marie-Claude Delahaye, the world expert on absinthe, to ensure total authenticity of his product. La Fée Absinthe was launched in 2000. The name reflects the spirit's historical nickname, 'the green fairy'. Traditionally, absinthe was green as a result of the post-distillation addition of herbs to strengthen the fragrance. Today the colour is as likely to result from artificial colouring, though such absinthes lack much of the characteristic herbal flavour of the traditional product. Mixed with water, the organic flavour compound, called anethole, is insoluble so the colour transforms into a cloudy, opalescent milky green, known as the *louche*.

Today, absinthe is produced in three distinct styles: distilled verte (green), distilled blanche (white) and cold compounded.

Reference to a Czech or Bohemian style of absinthe indicates that no anise or other traditional flavourings were employed in its production. Though high in alcohol and containing wormwood, this style of absinthe will not *louche*.

Absinthe is sometimes sweetened and is often described as a liqueur. But it's more properly defined as a strong, herbal spirit that is flavoured with botanicals either through distillation or cold compounding. Sometimes the word distilled on the label may refer only to the base spirit and the absinthe itself may be cold compounded. Traditionally, however, the botanicals are first macerated in the distillate and then the flavoured spirit is once or twice distilled.

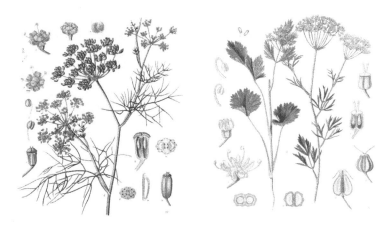

Fennel and anise side-by-side

The principle botanicals are grand wormwood (which grows throughout Europe on what is claimed to be the path that the exiled serpent took from the Garden of Eden), green anise and fennel. These are the so-called holy trinity but other botanicals are used in traditional absinthe production to reduce the bitterness of the oil extracted from the wormwood. These can include petite or Roman wormwood (primarily used for colouring), hyssop and lemon balm as well as small amounts of cinnamon, mint, coriander, angelica, star anise, juniper, nutmeg and gypsy weed.

ABSINTHE CLASSIFICATIONS

French absinthe is distilled. The botanicals are traditionally macerated in the spirit to generate the complex character before being redistilled. Chlorophyll may then be used to generate the emerald green colour. Large quantities of star anise and fennel are used to mask the bitter taste of wormwood and to ensure a full-bodied aniseed flavour combines with the strong citrus notes and rooty character drawn from angelica.

Preparing absinthe the traditional way. Note that no burning takes place.

Swiss absinthe is relatively scarce. This style uses less aniseed and more fennel. It is usually sweetened and bottled between 50% and 55% ABV.

Czech or Bohemian absinth is spelt without the 'e'. As Czechs never acquired a taste for anise, its flavour is less powerful though its alcohol levels can be relatively high. The colour is usually more electric blue than green and the product does not *louche*. The taste is comparatively bitter so these are absinthes that need to be sweetened with the ritual of burning sugar whereas the French tradition has always been to slowly pour four to six parts of iced water through sugar, placed on an absinthe spoon.

ANIS AND PASTIS

With absinthe banned in France in 1915, the Pernod factory temporarily closed. But in 1920 aniseed drinks were made legal again. Pernod introduced a new aniseed-flavoured drink *sans absinthe* (without absinthe) called anis. The Ricard Company followed with pastis. These products used many of the same ingredients as absinthe but the dried fruit of the Chinese star anise tree replaced the wormwood. This is an evergreen member of the magnolia family that is not to be confused with aniseed from the anise plant – a herb from the parsley family.

As both anis and pastis are flavoured with star anise and liquorice and both *louche*, many assume them to be variations of the same drink. However, anis is a mixture of a distillate of star anise and fennel with distillates of other aromatic plants and liquorice that is then sweetened and coloured.

To make pastis, a complex recipe of individual macerations takes place before blending with core distillates to deliver extra length and complexity. A maximum addition of 100 grams of sugar per litre is permitted. Anis tends to be more subtle in character and the dominant flavours are anise and herbs whereas liquorice tends to be more dominant in pastis.

RAKI AND OUZO

Raki is a non-sweet, anise-flavoured spirit distilled from various fruits, molasses or from grape pomace before sometimes being mixed with neutral alcohol. Popular in the Balkan regions, it is the national spirit of Turkey. Traditionally, it is relatively high in alcohol, usually between 40% and 50% ABV, but sometimes as high as 60% ABV. In the Balkans the term raki also refers to a non-anise-flavoured drink made from distilled pomace that is similar to Italian grappa.

Ouzo originated as a raki. The name ouzo was used only after certain shipments carried the Italian phrase *uso Massalia*, which means 'for commercial use, Marseille'. Today, it is probably the most famous Greek spirit, distilled from pressed grapes, berries and herbs, including aniseed, liquorice, mint and fennel. Some ouzos result from the distillation of the botanicals in a base spirit, while others come from a concentrated distillate of anise and fennel that is diluted with neutral spirit. Alcohol strength varies from 35% to 60% ABV. The taste is always dry, but some are softer and others richer.

ARRACK/ARACK/ARAK

Arrack is made in the Middle East and Asia but especially in Sri Lanka and Indonesia, from a variety of raw materials. Depending on its country of origin, the raw base material can be rice, palm sap, coconut flower, raisins or sugar cane. Flavourings can include herbs, spices and anise.

Arrack was originally brought to Europe by the Dutch East Indies Company. From the late seventeenth to the nineteenth century, punch was a popular celebratory drink in Europe and arrack was the most sought after base spirit; Jerry Thomas referenced arrack in his nineteenth-century *How to Mix Drinks* as an ingredient in Ruby Punch.

SAMBUCA

Distinct from the other Mediterranean anise-based liquors, sambuca is a neutral spirit that is infused with liquorice and elderberries, flavoured with anise and classified as a liqueur because it contains 350 grams of sugar per litre.

SCHNAPS/SCHNAPPS

Traditionally, schnaps was drunk as ice cold shots as part of a meal. Nowadays, it is a catch-all term for a range of white and flavoured spirits that are distilled from fermented fruit or grain in Germany, Austria and Switzerland. Its appearance and taste are varied though similar to eaux-de-vie, but this French term is seldom used in German-speaking countries.

In northern Germany the name schnaps is given to a popular

domestic white spirit, korn, which is almost always grain-based and pot distilled to retain the flavour of the raw material. It is bottled with no added sugar and at low strengths of around 32% ABV to be used as a base for mixers, or at 38% ABV and above for straight consumption. In southern Germany, Austria and Switzerland this spirit is more usually called obstler from the German for fruit, *Obst*. The fruits used are usually apples, pears, apricots, plums or cherries.

American schnapps results from mixing neutral grain spirit with fruit or other flavourings, adding sugar and, usually, glycerine to produce smooth, very sweet drinks. The alcohol content can be as low as 15% ABV. Because of their significant sugar content, technically these drinks fall into the liqueur category.

AKVAVIT/AQUAVIT

In Denmark, akvavit, and in Sweden, Norway and less so, in Finland, aquavit has for a long time been an important part of the local drinking culture. Distillation was initially from imported wine, but this was expensive. Now it is made from a mash of grain or potato, flavoured with macerations, diluted, redistilled like distilled gin, and then bottled, often at 45% ABV.

Regulations oblige the inclusion of caraway but other herbs, spices, or fruit oils may also be used. Usually it is a clear spirit, but some are aged and absorb more or less colour from the wood, depending on the type of wood and the amount of time it rests in the barrel. Use of caramel is permitted.

This spirit continues to account for a significant share of domestic sales in Scandinavia; traditionally enjoyed as a digestif it is also popular as an accompaniment to fish.

SOJU AND SHOCHU

Though both of these products are still very much national rather than international spirits, sales of one brand of soju are three times those of the biggest selling international spirit brand.

The Mongols probably acquired their distilling skills from the

Persians, introducing them into Korea when they invaded the region in the 1300s. The word soju is derived from the Chinese, but soju, the drink, is native to Korea.

It is clear in colour and tastes similar to vodka, though it is typically lower in strength and often slightly sweeter due to sugars being added during production. Though traditionally made from rice, most major brands supplement or even replace the rice with other starches from potato, wheat, barley, sweet potato or tapioca. It is usually consumed neat but often it will be used to give a kick to the local light beer and to provide a relatively mild alcoholic base to fruit juices and other mixers.

Although its origins were most likely in China, Thailand or Korea, shochu is native to Japan. The oldest reference is found in graffiti written by a carpenter in 1559 on the walls of a shrine in the city of Okuchi in the Japanese Prefecture of Kagoshima: 'I was disappointed that the manager didn't offer us a glass of shochu for all the hard work we've done for his shrine.' Today, Kagoshima is the only prefecture that produces no sake or spirit other than shochu. The production of honkaku shochu, with its emphasis on flavour and aroma, is particularly concentrated in this southern region of Japan.

The production of shochu can take from four months to one year to complete. Preparation of the first mash can take from three to four days or up to a month depending on the raw material, which could be rice, barley, buckwheat, sweet potato, or other more obscure ingredients. Each delivers different flavours, stretching from a smooth and lighter style using rice through nutty, fruity, floral and spicy styles to the strong, earthier style of potatoes.

Despite alcohol levels being relatively low, usually around 25% ABV, shochu is one of the more complex spirits. The choice of koji (a fungus used in fermentation) for the first mash of koji, water and yeast; selection of the raw materials to enter into the second mash; use of hard or soft water; and the choice of single or multiple distillation in wood or stainless steel will all influence the final product. The choice of white, black or yellow koji mould also impacts on flavour. White koji, the most popular, promotes rapid saccharification and results in a refreshing, gentle, sweet taste. Black koji extracts lots of character from the raw materials and results in rich aromas and a slightly sweet, mellow taste. Yellow koji results in a rich, fruity refreshing taste but it is rarely used as it can easily turn sour during fermentation in warmer regions.

The distillate is defined as honkaku (authentic) or otsurui (pot distilled) or kourui (column distilled). Maturation takes from one month to a year in earthenware containers, metal tanks, or wooden casks, adding distinctive flavours and aromas.

BAIJIU

Baijiu is a term used in Chinese to cover all distilled alcohol. It is a clear drink typically bottled between 40% and 60% ABV. Except for the rice used for rice baijiu, the raw material is usually sorghum, a member of the grass family. There are numerous styles, both flavoured and unflavoured.

Quiz on other flavoured white spirits

1. Who opened his first distillery in Couvet, Switzerland before changing his name to Pernod?

   A. Dr. Pierre Ordinaire
   B. Major Dubied
   C. M. Perrenoud
   D. None of these

2. Which of these ingredients is Artemisia absinthium, the key flavouring traditionally used in absinthe?

   A. Fennel
   B. Wormwood
   C. Anise
   D. Hyssop

3. Which of these statements, relating to absinthe, is true?

   A. The EU permits thujone levels of 10 ppm and the USA, 35 ppm

B. The EU and USA permit thujone levels of 10 ppm

C. The EU and USA permit thujone levels of 35 ppm

D. The EU permits thujone levels of 35 ppm and the USA, 10 ppm

4. In which of these countries were sales of absinthe never formally banned?

A. France

B. Belgium

C. Holland

D. United Kingdom

5. What is absinthe's historical nickname?

A. The green fairy

B. The green hour

C. The green sage

D. The green louche

6. When absinthe is mixed with water what insoluble flavour compound louches into a milky green colour?

A. Anethole

B. Chlorophyll

C. Artemisia

D. Thujone

7. Following the banning of absinthe, when were aniseed drinks made legal in France, permitting Pernod to introduce anis and Ricard, pastis?

A. 1905

B. 1915

C. 1920

D. 1925

8. From the late seventeenth to the nineteenth centuries what was the most celebrated ingredient in punch?

    A. Raki
    B. Arrack
    C. Ouzo
    D. Pastis

9. Akvavit is distilled in what country?

    A. Finland
    B. Norway
    C. Sweden
    D. Denmark

10. Shochu is native to which country?

    A. China
    B. Korea
    C. Japan
    D. Thailand

11. Soju is native to which country?

    A. Japan
    B. Korea
    C. China
    D. Thailand

12. Baijiu is a term used to describe distilled alcohol in which country?

    A. China
    B. Korea
    C. Malaysia
    D. Japan

1. C; 2. B; 3. D; 4. D; 5. A; 6. A; 7. C; 8. B; 9. D; 10. C; 11. B; 12. A.

Answers

8

RUM

DEFINITION OF RUM

Rum, *rhum* in French, *ron* in Spanish, or *aguardiente de cana* in Portuguese, is a product of sugar cane, either in the form of molasses or cane juice, fermented and distilled in a cane-growing country. Production of rum takes place throughout the tropical and sub-tropical world and both pot and continuous stills are permitted. Alcoholic strength must exceed 37% ABV in the EU, 40% ABV in the USA and higher strengths in some other countries. If labeled as overproof, the rums have to be bottled above 57% ABV. Colour varies from crystal clear, through pale straw, or *paille* in French, and various shades of gold to dark mahogany.

Sugar cane

Rum cannot be made from sugar beet and, though molasses may

be shipped from big producers in countries such as Guyana and Venezuela to another for distillation, the latter country must still be a cane grower. Only finished rums can be exported to non-cane-producing countries like Scotland or Germany, to be blended or aged. These are the only regulations governing rum production with the exception of some requirements that are specific either to producers or importers in individual countries.

HISTORY OF RUM

Thousands of years ago the Malay people fermented a drink from sugar cane called 'brum' or 'bram' and, in the fourteenth century, Marco Polo recorded sampling a 'very good wine of sugar'. According to some, the name is derived from 'rumbullion' meaning 'a great tumult or uproar' or from the large drinking vessels used by Dutch sailors, known as *roemers*. Others consider it to be a contraction of the Latin word for sugar, *saccharum*.

Rum is produced in almost all cane-growing countries, but the West Indies is recognized to be its home. There is also strong evidence that the name rum was first recorded there, in Barbados, in 1688. Certainly Europe's insatiable demand for sugar, the oil of its day, turned the Caribbean sugar plantations into some of the world's big profit earners, regrettably giving rise to the trade in African slaves shipped in to work the plantations.

During the production of sugar the crystals were removed, leaving behind dark, treacle-like molasses which still contained plenty of the sugar for fermentation to convert into alcohol and congeners for distillation to concentrate. Initially, this spirit was used to subdue the slave workers but slowly the molasses and the spirit began to be traded with other countries. Some European countries forbade imports from their colonies to protect their own domestic spirits. So their molasses were shipped to the new American colonies to be distilled there into rum and to become that country's first commercial spirit. Some molasses and some finished rums were also traded for more slaves in Africa.

In England, in the eighteenth century, after cognac had been banned and gin had become the choice of the urban poor, rum punch became the fashionable drink of the middle classes, looking to distinguish themselves from the poor.

During Prohibition in America the demand for authentic rums gave rise to a term still used today, 'The real McCoy', after the smuggler William McCoy who allegedly provided genuine, branded rums to clients willing to sail or steam to meet him in international waters off the coast of Florida.

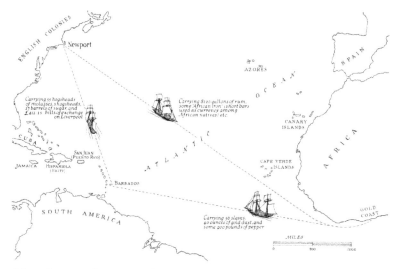

Map showing the triangular trade as illustrated by the voyage of the Sanderson, *sailing from Newport, RI, in March 1752*

THE ROYAL NAVY AND RUM

In the seventeenth century, spirits had replaced the Royal Navy's earlier ration of eight pints of beer per day because beer deteriorated quickly in the hot climates the navy was now patrolling. Rum's particularly strong links with the British Royal Navy began in 1655 when the Navy captured Jamaica. Until then brandy, shipped from Europe, had been the usual protection against pirates but Jamaican traders lobbied for rum to replace the daily issue of French brandy.

Their success, in 1687, saw the Royal Navy adopting a half pint of rum as a sailor's daily ration, a measure which reflected the previous allocation of beer.

The original 'tot' was a twice-daily issue of a quarter pint of neat rum, a quantity thought to be necessary to counteract the effects of salty, preserved meats and rancid cheese, not to say the difficult life on-board. The rum was likely to be as strong as 58% ABV but, despite this strength, it was drunk neat. In 1740, the Admiral of the Fleet, Admiral Vernon was so appalled by the drunkenness of the sailors that he insisted that water be issued with the rum.

Grog issue, circa 1905

His order required that the daily allowance of rum 'be every day mixed with the proportion of a quart of water to a half pint of rum, to be mixed in a scuttled butt kept for that purpose, and to be done upon the deck, and in the presence of the Lieutenant of the Watch who is to take particular care to see that the men are not defrauded in having their full allowance of rum... and let those that are good men receive extra lime juice and sugar that it be made more palatable to them.'

The admiral himself had become affectionately known as 'Old Grog' owing to the cloak he wore, made of a fabric called 'grogram'. Less affectionately, and because his watered down rum allocation offended sailors so much, they called it 'grog', a term still used today for a hot rum drink, as is the term 'groggy', to describe people who are unable to think clearly. The addition of lime, which was intended to help fight scurvy, gave rise to the nickname 'limeys', used ever since to describe British sailors.

Legend has it that before the Battle of Trafalgar, Admiral Lord Nelson ordered that, should he die, he wanted his body to be preserved in a barrel of rum until his ship arrived back in its home-port. So, upon his death, his body was placed in a barrel of rum. However, during the voyage home, the sailors drilled holes through the wood and drank the rum, giving rise to the British naval term for rum, 'Nelson's blood'.

It was not until 31 July 1970, 'Black Tot Day', that the Royal Navy rum ration was discontinued by the Admiralty and, by then, the Royal Navy operated in the nuclear age and the breathalyzer had been introduced.

HOW IS RUM MADE?

Rum is subject to very little regulation, resulting in it being the most varied of spirits, far removed from today's so-called global spirits, like vodka. Rum reflects local custom and is literally hand-crafted according to local tradition in tropical countries all around the world.

The individuality of rums can be influenced by many factors:

- The variety of sugar cane.

- The base product, i.e. cane juice or molasses.

- Climatic conditions.

- Terrain.

- Speed of fermentation and nature of yeast.

- Method of distillation and filtration.

- Local custom.

- Conditions of maturation.

- Length of ageing.

- Blending and colouring.

SUGAR CANE

Alexander the Great described sugar cane as the 'reed which gives honey without the help of bees'. This tropical grass probably originated in New Guinea and then spread to India (the process of making sugar by leaving the cane in the sun for the juice to evaporate was developed in India around 500BC), Malaysia and into the Pacific Islands before the Moors brought it to Europe. From there, the Dutch and the Spanish transplanted it to their colonies in South America and the Caribbean. It was on his second voyage, in 1493, that Christopher Columbus introduced sugar cane into Cuba.

Burning the sugar cane

Sugar cane can be harvested within six to eighteen months of being planted and re-harvested, with diminishing returns, for another six years. The cane may be cut mechanically or by hand. Traditionally, if being cut by hand, the plantations are first burnt to remove the sharp edged leaves and to clear the fields of dangerous animals and insects. The current trend towards mechanical harvesting removes this requirement. Most Caribbean islands harvest cane from February through June, but some may crop twice a year.

According to local tradition or through recent innovation, rum is distilled either directly from the juice of the crushed cane or from molasses, the thick treacle-like substance that remains once the sugar crystals have been boiled off and separated out.

MOLASSES

Fresh sugar cane is rich in sucrose and so there is no starch needing conversion into fermentable sugars. The cane need only be chopped and crushed by rollers and grinders to extract the cane juice and if this cane juice is fermented and the resulting 'grappe' or cane wine is distilled, the rum is called 'cane spirit' or *rhum agricole* on French-speaking islands.

To produce molasses-based rum or what is called *rhum industriel* on French-speaking islands, this juice must be concentrated through boiling, a process which crystallizes some of the sugars for extraction by centrifugal spinning.

Blackstrap molasses

As the process is repeated, more sugars are removed, leaving behind an increasingly dark, thick, black, treacle-like substance called blackstrap molasses. Molasses still consist mostly of sugar but, unlike refined sugars, they also contain large quantities of vitamins and minerals. Historically, rum producers used the molasses remaining after only two or three spins when still full of aromatic and flavoursome minerals and sugars. When demand for sugar increased, however, more spins were required and so less of these flavourful compounds remained in the molasses destined for rum production.

FERMENTATION

Molasses must be diluted to facilitate fermentation. Then, cultured or natural yeasts are added into the wash to convert the remaining sugars into alcohols. This stage is critical to the character of the finished rum. Depending on temperature, the nature of the yeast and the style of rum required, the process may be short, taking just a few hours or long, taking a number of days: the slower the process, the heavier the style of rum that emerges.

DUNDER

When the fermented mash is placed in the still, it contains practically all of the yeast cells, some living and some dead. After the alcohol has been removed by distillation these extracts remain, containing lots of concentrated minerals and other materials. These are collected and stored in a pit or tank under the hot Caribbean sun where the acids are concentrated and the pH level is reduced. Called dunder, these extracts are returned into a later fermentation as nourishment for the new yeast cells, to stimulate their growth and to help them to produce a larger yield. This action also slows down the rate of fermentation, contributing to the creation of a heavier and more pungent quality that is typical of some Jamaican rums.

DISTILLATION

Distillation can be in pot and/or continuous stills but, for rum, the spirit must exit the still below 96% ABV. Above that it will be classified as ethyl alcohol or ethanol and not as rum.

Usually a pot-still spirit will require two distillations, the first to around 70% ABV to define a rum's broad character and the second to refine the distillate but only to levels of alcohol which are low enough to retain much of the sugar cane's character. Typically, pot-still rums will be complex, heavy, pungent, aromatic and oily, usually requiring maturation to mellow before bottling. But much will depend upon the size and shape of the pot.

Pot still with retorts

Some pot stills incorporate retorts (the tanks in the centre of the photograph). These make it possible to double distil in one operation. Alcohol-rich vapours rise from the first pot and pass into the low wines retort that holds a mix of alcohol and water. The hot vapours cause the liquid in the retort to boil and release volatile flavour-laden vapours that then pass into the high wines retort where the process is repeated. The alcohol-rich vapours condense and, after a short run of heads, the middle cut is collected at around 85% ABV. The heads and tails are used to fill the retort for the next distillation. A short and early collection of spirit off the still results in lighter rums, while longer and later cuts result in richer, fuller-bodied, slightly oily rums.

A column still is normally associated with lighter rums and the production of a strong, pure spirit that is crisp, clean and dry with subtle aromas but little molasses character. However, a column still can be used to distil a full range of rum styles because alcohols may be collected off spirit plates set by the distiller anywhere in the rectifying column, at the exact temperatures where the required alcohols will condense.

All rum distillates exit water-white from both types of still.

MATURATION

Owing to their hot tropical climates, maturation in rum producing countries is rapid. If bottled as white, silver, or light rum, the distillate need not be aged, although some countries require all rums to be aged for minimum periods. Some white rums are rested in wood for a few months or as much as a year for the purpose of oxidation before the rum is filtered to remove any colour or character absorbed from the wood. Bacardí Limited calls this process 'dynamic filtration'.

Golden and dark rums are aged to gain colour and character from the wood, usually, but not always, in once-used, ex-bourbon barrels. Most distillers then employ burnt sugar to adjust the final colour of their rum. Some styles of rum, such as 'navy', use burnt sugar to contribute to the taste as well, while others may use it to mask a lack of significant maturation in wood.

Paille is a French term used to describe pale, straw-coloured *rhum* that has been aged in oak casks from twelve to eighteen months to make it smoother than unaged *rhum blanc*.

If maturation takes place in Europe, such as in Scotland, where it is cool and damp, improvements in the barrel are slow but annual evaporation losses are also low at around 2%. In the tropics, where it is hot and humid, maturation is three times faster, but as much as 6% can be lost annually through evaporation. This increases the scarcity value of rums aged in such countries.

So to judge the value of an aged rum, it is important to know where the rum has been aged and what the local custom may be. In ex-British colonies any stated age is the minimum. Latin country producers think this fails to reflect the true character of their blended rums and so may declare an average age or execute maturation via a solera system, replacing older spirit drawn from one barrel with younger spirit drawn from another so that the younger draws influence from the nature of the older rums.

The requirement for maturation depends very much on decisions taken with regard to fermentation and distillation. Pot-still rums usually need longer to mature than those from a column still. Regulations in individual countries, may also define minimum maturation periods.

BLENDING

Most rums are blends of distillates that are produced to different alcohol levels, maybe from both pot and column stills, possibly aged for more or less time and perhaps in different wood types, maybe selected from different regions and some, even from different countries. So a rum company's most valuable asset is the master blender, whose skills and traditions are jealously guarded secrets that ensure consistency, individuality and style in the final blend.

Massive stocks are used to complete the blending operation in large tanks before the rum is returned to barrels for further maturation. When tasting, one rule of thumb is that the richer the aromatics and flavour, the higher the likely percentage of pot-distilled rum.

REDUCTION

Finally, the spirit is reduced to the required strength for bottling; usually this is 37.5%, 40%, or 43% ABV, but to satisfy demand for higher strength, overproof rums are bottled above 57% ABV.

The quality of water used is important and sometimes a distiller may even attribute particular values to the water, for instance, if the water's drawn from underground springs.

COLOURING

All spirit off the still is colourless but it is quite common for consumers to associate colour with strength, so white rums are thought to be weaker than dark rums. In fact, nothing could be further from the truth. Colour in rum may result from colour drawn from wood during maturation but it may also result from the addition of burnt sugar.

TYPICAL STYLES FOUND IN SOME RUM-PRODUCING COUNTRIES

Rums are produced around the world: in Australia, in India and on islands in the Indian Ocean, in the Philippines and on other Pacific Islands, in Africa and in South and Central America. However, the Caribbean alone, measuring 1,500 square miles, produces a greater variety of rums than any other region, and they are as varied in style as the number of Caribbean islands and countries themselves.

The word 'Caribbean' derives from the Carib Indians, their language and culture. So Caribbean refers to the areas historically inhabited by the Carib Indians, including the Carib-inhabited islands and the countries that surround the Caribbean Sea such as Nicaragua and others in eastern Central America as well as Colombia and Venezuela in northern South America. Though there are exceptions, most countries have gained their reputations with certain individual styles.

Lighter, golden rum

Anguilla's early reputation stemmed from The Planters Rum Company, but Prohibition closed it down. Sugar cane was never a big crop and now the island imports and blends pot-still rums, aged in American and French oak, to produce soft, medium bodied and spicy rums.

Antigua uses pot and column stills to distil rum from imported molasses and the dry climate provides an excellent ageing environment.

Barbados employs pot and column stills as well as proprietary yeasts to produce sweetish, molasses-based rums for ageing in small barrels. The rums are full of vanilla and fruit, heavier and more flavourful than rums from many other islands and so are ideal for mixing in punches. Bajan rum must be matured for at least one year. Mount Gay was first produced in 1703, which possibly makes this the oldest brand of rum in the world. Here too is R L Seale, one of the newest distillers in the Caribbean, using modern techniques such as vacuum distillation to avoid overcooking.

Bermuda has no distilleries or cane fields and so imports and blends rums on the island. Goslings Black Seal, the most famous of this island's rums, is the base spirit for the famous Dark 'n' Stormy cocktail.

Powerful, molasses-based rum

Guyana uses pot and column stills and is justly famous for its rich, heavy Demerara rums, named after the local river. The sweetish, full-bodied rums can be matured for many years, either in the Caribbean or in Europe. Some are bottled as Guyana rums while many others are blended with lighter rums from other countries or shipped in bulk to Europe for blending into navy style rums that are dark in colour and heavy in body.

Pungent, high-ester rum

Jamaica produces full-bodied, rich, dark, pungent rums, retaining lots of underlying molasses flavour from the pot still. Unusually, some Jamaican rums are still fermented and distilled on the estates where the cane is grown and these are called 'estate rums'. Appleton's provides typical examples of the rich, fruity, spicy rums that age on this island plus some of the lighter golden styles that appeared in the latter part of the twentieth century, to attract drinkers who were denied their whiskies in America during and after Prohibition.

Light, molasses-based rum

Trinidad is the home of Angostura, the founder's sons having moved production from Venezuela in 1875. During the 1930s, the company began to make its own rum and alcohol for the famous bottled bitters. Traditionally, this island tended to produce rums with plenty of fusel oils and lots of oak flavour but now it also produces and blends lighter, molasses-based, column-still rums. A recent initiative is the production of an *agricole*-style rum.

French Island (mostly) *rhum agricole*

Guadeloupe uses the column still to produce mainly the typical French style of *rhum agricole*. During the early harvest some cane juice from the sugar mill is available for production of this style of *rhum*. Only when the juice is no longer available is the molasses fermented to make *rhum industriel*.

Rhum agricole is typically strong in fruit and full of herbal aromas. The style varies from *blanc* (white), which is rested for a few months, and *ambre* (gold), to the styles that are aged in used French or American casks; these are known as *vieux* (old), aged for a minimum of three years, *hors d'âge* (beyond age) and vintage. Some compare well with high quality French brandies. Martinique was where Père Labat landed in 1694 and where he introduced the latest advances in distillation. It was here that the Dillons, Empress Josephine's family, founded the oldest distillery and another, La Mauny, is the largest distillery in the French West Indies. The island has the largest number of distilleries in the eastern Caribbean, using pot and column stills to produce *rhum agricole* and *rhum industriel*. *Rhum agricole* must be produced according to AOC (appellation d'origine contrôlée) regulations laid down by the French. These regulations permit no addition of flavourings.

Haiti produces heavy, pot-still rums, aged in oak casks to develop smooth, full flavoured styles such as Barbancourt. Haiti also has an extensive underground industry to supply the needs of voodoo and religious ritual practitioners.

Hispanic, lighter, white and golden rums

Cuba was where Columbus introduced the sugar cane into the Caribbean in 1493, describing the island as 'the most beautiful land I have ever seen'. The variety of cane used in Cuba today remains unique to the island. Easy access for Americans during Prohibition was the key to establishing rum, and particularly Cuban rum, as an essential ingredient in many popular cocktails, though it is now illegal to ship Cuban rums into the United States. The rum, all distilled in column stills, is typically light-bodied, grassy, crisp and clean. Havana Club and Santiago both provide fine examples of the island's styles.

The Dominican Republic is notable for its full-bodied aged white and gold rums, distilled from molasses in column stills. Brugal and Matusalem rums are fine examples of this island's style. Some, like

Matusalem, use the solera system for blending rums as they age. Rums withdrawn from one barrel for bottling are replaced with younger rums in a process that stretches back to new spirit, fresh from the still. A solera number on the label will not represent the age of the youngest rum in the blend.

Puerto Rico is home to Bacardí Limited, which began to move its operations from Cuba to Puerto Rico in the 1930s. All the rum produced on this island is column distilled from molasses. Most rums are characteristically light and, even though all must be aged in wood for at least one year, much of the rum is filtered after ageing to remove any of the colour and character that is absorbed from the wood.

Venezuela's tropical location, altitude and rainfall generate higher levels of sugar than any other region in the world. The country distils such a large quantity of different rums that identifying one single style as being typical is not possible. Santa Teresa and Cacique are examples of two varying styles. Taste can be close to the Cuban style, but a typical trait for this country and South America in general is a heavy sweetness that can often mask the alcohol. Regulations require a minimum of two years of ageing in oak barrels to merit the designation 'ron'. In 2004, Ron de Venezuela was granted global recognition as a beverage of distinctive quality that is created in a unique region.

The Virgin Islands are divided between the United States and the British. These islands employ mainly column stills to produce light bodied rums from imported molasses. Cruzan is the largest seller in these islands while the Arundel Estate is the oldest continuously operated distillery in the eastern Caribbean, combining cane juice, a long and natural fermentation and single pot distillation to produce a truly unique rum. Pusser's rum, born out of the British naval tradition of a daily ration of rum, is a blend of Caribbean rums, bottled on Tortola in the British Virgin Islands.

Australian rum

Australian rum became an important currency in the early days of the colony of New South Wales. It was valuable as local coinage and for its ability to provide temporary relief from the lack of creature comforts in the emerging colony. Today Australia produces flavoursome, full-bodied rums from large sugar estates in Queensland.

Navy rum

Navy rums do not technically exist but the term, 'navy' is a description used to suggest a heavy style of rum, historically associated with the British Royal Navy. Heavy caramel is evident not only in the colour but also in the taste. A donation from the sales of one navy-style rum, Pusser's, is given to a naval charity, The Royal Navy Sailor's Fund.

German & Austrian 'rum'

Rum-verschnitt (literally meaning 'blended rum') is produced in Germany as a low-cost substitute for genuine dark rum and was particularly popular between the wars. It is a blend of genuine high-ester Jamaican rum, rectified spirit, water and caramel colouring. By law, the rum must represent a minimum of 5% of the liquid volume. The taste remains similar to that of true dark rum.

Inländer rum is similar, but produced in Austria and is sometimes called 'domestic rum'.

CACHAÇA

This spirit, a speciality of Brazil, is distilled from cane juice and widely consumed in South America. Sugar cane was introduced into what was to become Brazil in 1505 and shortly after, in 1533, the first sugar mills were built and production of cachaça followed, more than a century before the first record of rum in the Caribbean.

The production of cachaça was probably inspired by a combination of the prohibitive cost of shipping brandy from Europe to the colonies and a commercial desire, first on the part of Portugal and then the Dutch, to compete with the profitable European trade that had been created and driven by imports of arrack from the East. Soon, however, cachaça, like tequila in Mexico, became a symbol of resistance and revolution for the many slaves that had arrived in Brazil from West Africa, helping these poorest of people to forget their poverty. A rough translation of the word *cachaça* is 'burning water'. The word *caipira* means 'farmer'. So the caipirinha, the drink chosen by today's marketeers to drive cachaça beyond Brazil, is close to cachaça's heritage, rather than just being a drink created by marketeers for the fashionistas.

Certainly cachaça's success was very evident by the eighteenth century because local taxes imposed on cachaça by the Portuguese were a major contributor towards the reconstruction of Lisbon after the 1755 earthquake.

Though virtually unknown outside Brazil until the 1980s, over 35,000 commercial brands are now produced by around 17,000 distillers. Annual production exceeds one billion litres, making cachaça the third largest white spirit in the world behind soju and vodka. More cachaça is drunk in Brazil than rum is on a global scale.

Cachaça is a trademark owned by the Brazilian producers who use it for export purposes.

Cachaça production

The largest production area is São Paulo and industrial-scale production in the large-scale mills is mostly located here and in Ceara. Both use continuous distillation to retain only the higher alcohols and esters and so retain less of any distinctive character from the sugar cane. Much of this production is sold in bulk to the bottlers of brands. Across Brazil, however, thousands of large and small pot stills are used to produce artisanal cachaça.

The spirit is not distilled from molasses, but from the juice of unrefined sugar cane. This juice must be freshly pressed from the cane within twenty-four hours of harvest so distilleries are sited near cane plantations. Fermentation may start naturally in open vats or be stimulated by the addition of a maize and rice-based yeast to provide extra protein to the growing yeast culture and to add distinctive flavour and aroma to the finished spirit. Use of these non-sugar products distinguishes cachaça from rum.

Compared with 65%– 5% ABV for a typical *rhum agricole*, cachaça must be distilled to no higher than 54% ABV and bottled between 38 and 48% ABV, parameters set by the government to ensure cachaça retains the scent and flavour of the sugar cane. Some producers may distil to nearer bottling strength. Total content of congeners, before dilution, is between 2,000 ppm and 6,500 ppm, more than will be found in many rums. Some producers add up to six grams of sugar per litre before bottling and, if no more than six grams are added, no mention is made on the label.

Though classified as a white spirit, some producers age their cachaça in barrels, cut from a wide variety of native trees, many of which contribute additional and unique flavours. Some age their product in barrels, holding as few as 200 litres, while others age in tanks holding more than 50,000 litres.

Styles of cachaça

- **White cachaças** are clear and usually unaged, though some may rest for up to sixty days before bottling.

- **Abocada cachaças** may contain from six to thirty grams of sugar per litre but no reference to this needs to be made on the labels.

- **Aromatized cachaças** carry no legal definition, but these are infused or aromatized with the likes of fruits, herbs and spices.

- **Aged cachaças** are matured for no less than one year in 700 litre wooden barrels to acquire notes of cinnamon, nutmeg, honey and dried fruit. Regulations specify that a bottle of aged cachaça must contain at least 50% wood-matured spirit. Within the aged category, cachaça premium must be aged in 700 litre barrels for more than one year, while cachaça extra premium must be aged in 700 litre barrels for more than three years.

Woods used to age cachaça

Oak trees are not native to Brazil so American oak and French oak in the form of ex-cognac and wine barrels are imported to add colour and additional character to the new spirit. But carvalho and many other indigenous woods are also widely used to age cachaça; these include an aromatic cherry wood (amburana), wood from the 'giant of the forest' (jequitiba), a peanut tree (amendoim), a walnut tree (freijo) and an ash tree (garapa), none of which impart much colour. Wood from the angelim-araroba tree imparts lots of character and colour; the balsamo and cabreuva trees plus a Brazilian chestnut tree (castanheira) all add colour, character and aromatics. A member of the laurel family (louro) is used for distinctive spicy notes. The yellow ipe, source of Brazil's national flower, imparts softness and an orange colour. It should be noted that the use of indigenous woods has prompted concerned producers to recognize a need to protect Brazil's virgin rain forest from less scrupulous operators.

Quiz on rum and cachaça

1. Rum is the product of what raw material?

    A. Sugar cane juice
    B. Sugar cane juice and molasses
    C. Sugar molasses
    D. Sugar beet

2. 'Overproof' means the rum's strength must exceed what level of alcohol?

    A. 45% ABV
    B. 53% ABV
    C. 57% ABV
    D. 60% ABV

3. In what year did Christopher Columbus introduce sugar cane cuttings into Cuba?

    A. 1409
    B. 1437
    C. 1475
    D. 1493

4. Which Caribbean island claims to have first used the term 'rum' to describe their sugar-can spirit?

    A. Jamaica

B. Barbados

C. Cuba

D. Trinidad

5. When did the admiralty discontinue the daily rum ration to the British Royal Navy?

A. 31 July 1890

B. 31 July 1910

C. 31 July 1940

D. 31 July 1970

6. Which of these phrases is a correct description of *rhum industriel*?

A. Must be produced from molasses

B. Must be produced in French territories

C. Must be produced from cane sugar

D. Must be produced in column stills

7. To be called 'rum' a spirit must exit the still below what level of alcohol?

A. 72% ABV

B. 84% ABV

C. 94% ABV

D. 96% ABV

8. *Paille* is a French term used to describe what style of rum?

A. Aged white rum

B. Aged pale straw rum

C. Unaged gold rum

D. A rum blend

9. The climate of which country generates the world's highest level of sugar?

A. Guyana

B. Australia

C. Venezuela

D. India

10. Which of these rums is one of, if not the oldest, rum in the world?

A. Mount Gay

B. Appleton

C. Bacardí

D. Goslings

11. Which of these countries produces Demerara rums?

A. Bermuda

B. US Virgin Islands

C. Guadeloupe

D. Guyana

12. Rums from which of these islands must be produced according to AOC regulations?

A. Martinique

B. Anguilla

C. Haiti

D. Puerto Rico

13. Cachaça is the speciality spirit of which country?

A. Colombia

B. Brazil

C. Mexico

D. Peru

14. Cachaça is usually distilled to between what levels of alcohol?

A. 37.5%–40% ABV

B. 45%–60% ABV

C. 48%–52% ABV

D. No limits

15. Aged cachaça must be matured in what minimum size of barrels?

   A. 500 litres
   B. 600 litres
   C. 700 litres
   D. 800 litres

16. Which of these statements is not true?

   A. Cachaça was in production before rum
   B. A bottle of aged cachaça must contain at least 50% wood-matured spirit
   C. Juice for cachaça must be pressed from cane within 24 hours of harvest
   D. Cachaça is the world's largest selling spirit

17. Which rum is born out of the tradition of issuing a daily ration of rum to sailors?

   A. Gosling's
   B. Pusser's
   C. Brugal
   D. Cacique

18. In which of these styles of rum would caramel be noticeable in the colour and the taste?

   A. Navy rum
   B. Australian rum
   C. Solera rum
   D. Demerara rum

19. Which of these statements is true of rum maturation in the tropics?

   A. Evaporation losses can be as low as 2%

B. Maturation can be much slower than in cooler climates
C. Early evaporation losses can be as high as 6%
D. The spirit must be matured in a solera system

MAKING COCKTAILS WITH RUM

Of all the spirits available to the budding cocktailian, rum is possibly the most exciting. The breadth and diversity of styles available, often reflecting the climate, history and production techniques unique to its country and distillery, alongside a fairly laissez-faire attitude to regulation, mean that simple recipes have extraordinary scope for variation. From the molasses-based, darkest of dark, black navy rums to overproof white rhum agricoles, via a glorious variety of aged rums, bottled from three to twenty five years old and more, there is a rum to suit almost any drink style and, importantly, all budgets.

The Daiquiri

In one of the most elementary pieces of cocktail invention ever documented, in 1896 a mining engineer by the name of Jennings Cox 'created' the Daiquiri in the eponymous mining town in the north of Cuba. Since his creation involved mixing Cuban rum with locally grown limes and sugar and nothing else, it was very unlikely that this had not been done myriad times before but the name stuck. One of the main reasons why this drink is part of the cocktail lexicon is that Prohibition in the USA had the side effect of making Havana one of the premier holiday destinations for Americans looking to party.

The rums of Cuba are unique in style, gentle and refined, pioneered by Bacardi's innovations in distillation and particularly their use of filtration to produce a white rum with character and fewer impurities. This smooth character was quite a departure from other island rum styles and means Cuban rums can form the basis of a whole family of crisp citrus driven cocktails.

50ml rum
20ml lime juice
20ml simple syrup (see page 95)

Shake all ingredients with ice, hard! Strain into a chilled cocktail glass and garnish with a wedge of lime split and placed on the glass rim. The Daiquiri is all about personal taste, with the perfect balance of sweet and sour a truly individual choice. For this reason feel free to alter the amounts of sugar and lime juice to achieve the desired levels. When serving a guest who's prelidections are not known, use the recipe above, which is slightly sweet. The drinker can then easily adjust by squeezing a few drops of lime from the wedge garnish.

The original drink uses a light Cuban rum but feel free to use *any* rum, of *any* style. More than any other drink the Daiquiri provides a reference point for the spirit used, permitting real evaluation of the character of the rum. Try a comparison between similarly aged products from different islands or a range of ages from the same distiller. Each will produce different Daiquiris. The only unifying factor will be that they will all be delicious. Experimentation needn't stop there. Wonderful Daiquiris can be made with the addition of aromatic bitters to the recipe, the substitution of honey, maple syrup or flavoured sugars for the simple syrup and, of course, the addition of almost any ripe fruit.

The Mojito

After the Daiquiri, Cuba's other great contribution to mixology is the Mojito. Sir Francis Drake supposedly enlivened the rum ration of the navy with limes and mint to make the sometimes raw rums encountered throughout the Caribbean more palatable and it could be said that this was the first Mojito. Others suggest that American customers, used to their Mint Juleps, asked for similar drinks. The Mojito proper requires a rum of finesse to work with the fresh flavours of mint and lime and so the drink was truly born in the great bars of Havana. Now one of the world's most popular cocktails, the Mojito can be constructed in a number of ways, depending on the provisions available, particularly the style and quality of ice. In Cuba the drink is often served in a fashion akin to a rum Mint Collins. Rum, sugar, lime and mint are left to infuse for half an hour, cubed ice is added and the drink is topped with soda. This is great when serving large groups like a tour party from a cruise ship but less good for making individual drinks. The recipe below is one arrived at after much practice.

50ml light rum
25ml lime juice
25ml simple syrup (see page 95)
8 mint leaves
40ml soda water

Place the mint leaves in the bottom of a large highball glass and gently crush them briefly with a pestle or cocktail muddler. The essential oils are volatile so take care not to do more than bruise the leaves. The drink does not benefit from too many broken leaf membranes. Add the rum, lime juice and sugar and half the glass of cracked ice and churn thoroughly to mix. Fill the glass with cracked ice and add the soda water. Garnish with a mint sprig and a lime wedge.

Great Mojitos can be made with a variety of styles of rum, although the herbaceous flavour of light Spanish island rums produces the most authentic version and works amazingly with the menthol notes. You can certainly use lightly aged rums from all over the Caribbean and there are advocates of adding a dash of bitters or even using dark rum. Be brave and experiment!

The Caipirinha

The Caipirinha is the national drink of Brazil, literally translated as 'little farmer's drink'. The drink relies on Brazil's national spirit, cachaça which is similar to a *rhum agricole*, made not only from the juice of sugar cane but also from some of the vegetal remains of the cane after milling. This raw material, combined with the low distillation proof results in a spirit containing a high proportion of aromatic esters and tasting like nothing else.

50ml cachaça
1 whole lime
1 tsp unrefined sugar
15–20ml simple syrup (see page 95)

Cut almost through the lime from pole to pole and slice 8–10 lines of latitude, again almost through the body of the lime to make something that looks a little like a rib cage. Open slightly and put the granulated sugar inside. This will help extract the oils and juice from the lime. Carefully crush the fruit with a large pestle and add the rest of the ingredients and swizzle. As each lime delivers a unique amount of juice, check the balance is pleasing and then fill the glass with crushed ice, swizzle and serve.

Voodoo Rum Punch

No chapter on rum would be complete without a rum punch recipe. Developed over the last twenty years, this Voodoo Rum Punch has elements of Tiki culture in its use of a blend of rums, and takes advantage of the huge array of tropical fruits and juices now commonly available. The recipe below is a guide. Feel free to adapt as required. The quantities below will make approximately sixty drinks and should be served in a very large punch bowl or tapped demi-john.

1 bottle Woods 100 overproof dark rum
1 bottle good quality white rum
2 bottles good quality anejo rum
1 bottle Wray and Nephew white overproof rum
1 bottle orange curacao
1 bottle passionfruit syrup
200ml Falernum syrup
1.5l fresh lemon juice
24 fresh passionfruits
1l mango puree
3l guava juice
3l pressed apple juice
30 dashes Angostura bitters

Scoop out the flesh of the passion fruits and place in a large punch bowl. Add all the rest of the ingredients and chill for an hour. The best method is to fill an old ice cream tub, or similar, with water and freeze overnight to produce a large single block of ice, which is placed in the punch bowl with the rest of the ingredients. Just before service add slices of lime, pineapple and orange and serve with a ladle, in large cups with extra ice and umbrellas.

9

BRANDY

BRANDY BACKGROUND

Brandies can be distilled wherever grapes are grown. They can be divided into two categories: grape brandies, which are distilled from fermented grape juice and pomace brandies such as grappa and marc, which are distilled from the pressed pulp and skin. French grape brandy is an exception as it is made from neutral spirit blended with high-proof grape spirit. Fruit brandies distilled from fruits other than grapes must specify the fruit.

Unlike other spirits, brandy's supremacy has never been in any doubt.

HISTORY OF COGNAC

The Romans first planted vines in southwest France but the wines from this region only became popular in the Middle Ages, after the marriage of the Norman King Henry II to Eleanor of Aquitaine in 1152. The 300 years of English rule that followed across the whole of southwest France led to a British thirst for wines from this region and from Bordeaux in particular. The town of Cognac's position on the River Charente, near the port of La Rochelle provided easy access for boats. The Dutch, who had become the world's dominant trading nation, first shipped white wines from the chalky slopes located here on the south bank of the Charente opposite Cognac in 1549. Later that century, they discovered these rather ordinary and very acidic wines were ideal for distillation and, unlike others that required numerous distillations to become palatable, the wines from the Charente required only two distillations to be transformed into a quality distillate.

As they sailed the oceans with this *brandewijn*, they discovered that its quality improved in wood. Cognac gained a reputation for its undoubted superiority to other spirits and became the choice of the rich and powerful throughout the world.

When the aristocrats of late seventeenth-century London took to 'coniack brandy', its fame was assured, and when war interrupted Dutch trading from 1701 to 1713 not only was the brandy able to age longer in wood, but other nationalities were free to take an interest in this region's produce. Jean Martell arrived from Jersey in 1715; Richard Hennessy from Ireland in 1765; and Thomas Hine from England in 1791. Unfortunately, a bug from America that had not survived the long Atlantic crossings by sail arrived in France courtesy of the early steam ships. In the 1870s this phylloxera aphid destroyed all the cognac vines. It took twenty years to repair the damage. This provided plenty of opportunity for gin and blended scotch to capture the market. Fortunately cognac's unique qualities and its capacity to age ensured that, in time, it did regain recognition but more as the supreme brandy of brandies than as the global spirit of choice.

Today four firms, Martell, Hennessy, Courvoisier and Rémy Martin, account for 80% of total sales. These brands, along with every other reputable firm, produce their own distinctive styles of cognac. All cognacs are brandies but all brandies are certainly not cognacs.

COGNAC REGIONS

The Cognac region, situated in the Charente and Charente-Maritime departments, north of Bordeaux and near the French Atlantic coast, was first classified by geologist Professor Coquand, who visited the region in 1860 and analyzed its many different soils and sub-soils. He divided the region into six areas according to the differing soils and microclimates: cooler to the north, warmer to the south, maritime towards the sea, humid by the river and continental towards the Massif Central.

The Cognac region was classified by official decree on 1 May 1909 and was defined with greater delineation over the following thirty years. These regions remain the key to the individuality of cognac, as well as to defining cognac's superiority over all other brandies. Even when distillation and maturation are identical, grapes from these different areas contribute different characters to their respective distillates. The bigger firms, keen to gain loyalty for their particular brand names, prefer not to sell brandies made from individual regions but a handful of merchants and an increasing number of distillers do emphasize the geographical origin of their brandies.

The chalk slopes situated south of Cognac are called Champagne, but this has nothing to do with the area located nearly 400 miles to the north-east. Rather, the word comes from the Latin for light and chalky soil.

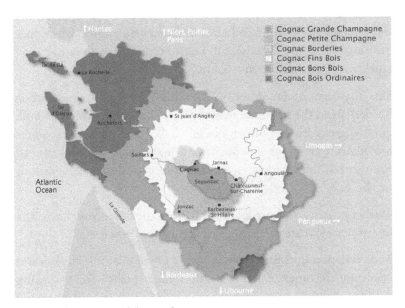

Map of the Cognac delimited region

Grande Champagne accounts for approximately 18% of this AOC (appellation d'origine contrôlée). This is the most prestigious area, rich in thick campanian chalk slopes and sheltered from the westerly winds. The region is south of the town of Cognac. Grapes here are full of acidity and produce the best cognacs, delicate and elegant but needing more than fifteen years of maturation to reach their best.

Petite Champagne accounts for approximately 21% of this AOC region. It is an area of santonian chalk, so-called because of the historical name for the area. These brandies are influenced more by a combination of the warmer inland climate to the east and colder maritime weather to the west. They are less intense, more floral and mature more quickly.

Fine Champagne is not an area but a description of cognac made only from the two Champagne areas, with at least 50% coming from the Grande Champagne.

Borderies accounts for approximately 5% of this AOC region, the smallest area that lies to the north and west of Cognac. Here, the soil contains more flint and clay. Grapes ripen earlier to produce the most distinctive, intense, full-bodied brandies that mature more quickly and give guts to any blend.

Fins Bois accounts for around 42% of this AOC region, surrounding Borderies and the two Champagne areas. The area provides the bulk of all cognac. Its soft brown glacial chalk, sand and clay produce heavier fruity, fragrant and quick maturing cognacs, the backbone of younger bottlings. However, the area is huge and so generalizations are difficult.

Quality cognacs now use grapes only from the four areas above. The two areas below are increasingly marginal and vine-free.

Bons Bois accounts for approximately 12% of this AOC region and surrounds the outer edges of Fins Bois. Here quality declines owing to the predominance of sand but exceptions can be found where the soil is more chalky.

Bois Ordinaires makes up approximately 2% of this AOC region. The area borders the sea and includes the islands of Ré and Oléron. Here, the chalk gives way almost entirely to sand and the influence of the sea is considerable. The cognac is relatively quick maturing with distinct maritime influences such as hints of salt and algae.

COGNAC GRAPES

Climate in all the areas is relatively mild. Grapes rarely ripen and so retain their acidity. The wines are thin and sour providing poor quality table wine. However these same characteristics mean they are ideal for distillation.

The Ugni Blanc grape

In the Cognac region grape juice is integral to the finished spirit but not as important as it is for wine. The balance of fruit and acidity in the grape is more important than the grape's flavour. Too much flavour and the brandy will be unbalanced. A few acres are planted with Folle Blanche and Colombard grapes, both very popular before the phylloxera blight and both able to provide attractive aromatics to any blend. Today the dominant grape, accounting for around 98% of production, is the white, neutral, late-ripening Ugni Blanc, also called Saint Emilion or Trebbiano. This grape is chosen, even for such a northerly region, because of its neutrality, relative lack of sugar and high acidity even at harvest time

The acidity minimizes the fruit content in the wine and reduces the level of sugar available for conversion into alcohol. But a late ripener like Ugni Blanc also reduces the time for wines to go stale between fermentation and distillation. The acidity provides a natural preservative to keep the wines fresh. This is important given that regulations governing production of cognac do not permit any use of the sulphur dioxide used elsewhere to protect wines from unwanted bacterial infection. High acidity and low levels of sugar also result in a relatively low and acidic wine alcohol of around 9% ABV. When this is distilled to 72% ABV, the alcohol and the flavours held within the alcohol are concentrated as many as eight times. More sugar in the grapes delivers a higher initial strength and permits less concentration during distillation, resulting in flat and flabby cognacs.

Grapes are pressed immediately but not too fiercely to avoid the transfer of too much undesirable character from the pips and skins. Fermentation takes place with no added sugar or sulphur dioxide and averages around five days. The wines may be racked off their lees (decomposed yeast cells and grape sediment) or left for distillation *sur lie* (on the lees).

COGNAC PRODUCTION

By December, most wines are ready for distillation; by law, wines for cognac must be distilled before the 31st March following the harvest to retain their freshness and aromatic esters. Some producers distil on the lees to increase richness and complexity in their cognacs. But in these cases, the extra congeners that remain in the distillate require longer maturation.

Distillation, a process little changed since the early eighteenth century, is executed in batches in a traditional, alembic, Charentais pot still made of copper. Heat comes from a naked flame, now usually natural gas because gas is easy to control. The bulbous head and short neck allow vapours full of impurities to flow through the swan's neck down into a coiled pipe called the *serpentin*. There, the vapours cool and condense into the concentrated distillate which evolves into the complex character of aged cognac. Some newer stills are taller to deliver the less rich spirit required for more neutral tasting brandies.

The first distillation produces a *brouillis* of about 30% ABV. Although many of the elements that define a cognac's final quality have already been created, these need to be refined. The size of the pot used for the first distillation has grown over the years. But the pot used for the second distillation, *la bonne chauffe*, must, by law, hold no more than twenty-five hectolitres, equal to around 3,000 bottles. The second distillation serves to concentrate, refine, select and discard.

Alembic

Stills may not vary much in shape but the distiller can and does choose where to make cuts to control the nature of the distillate. If the raw spirit continues to be drawn off at lower strengths, the cognac's character is richer and more complex. If the tap is switched off earlier, at a higher strength, a light, relatively neutral, drier spirit results. The difference may not be so great at first, but it shows in later years.

'Heads', the first few litres of spirit drawn off the still during the second distillation, are above the legal limit of 72% ABV and so these are removed. The strength of the heart of the distillate drops to around 60%, after which flow the *secondes*. Some distillers return these into the wine prior to distillation, increasing alcoholic strength and reducing the potential for concentration. Others add these into the *brouillis* (a low alcohol, cloudy liquid) to deliver a fruitier style of distillate. Others may return one part to the wine and the other to the *brouillis* to achieve their specific house style.

Newly distilled cognac is aromatic but unpalatable, not only because of its strength but because it lacks balance. Only maturation mellows the character and balances the distillate through the physical and chemical processes of oxidation, evaporation and absorption of tannin and vanillin from the oak barrels.

MATURATION

The creation of Cognacs requires patience, taking up to fifty years. They need time for a natural reduction of strength and to create their complex concentration of flavour. This maturation process is also costly, as around 3%, the 'angel's share', evaporates from the casks each year.

Wood for the casks is chosen carefully. It is sourced either from Limousin, 100 miles to the east of Cognac or from the forest of Tronçais, 150 miles north-east of Limoges. Both woods are used by custom rather than regulation. Initially, Limousin timber was the only wood available and it was simply floated down the river Charente to Cognac. However, the construction of railways enabled alternative supplies of wood to be sourced from the forest of Tronçais, first planted in the seventeenth century to provide wood for the French navy.

Limousin has a loose, fat grain, (much more so than Tronçais), allowing more transfer of air into the cask and more tannins into the distillate. These tannins provide the colour and because the oak is porous, in time they help to mellow the spirit. Maturation for many years in this wood contributes rich complexities to the cognac.

Tronçais is tighter grained, less porous and contains fewer tannins and more lignins. This wood is used more for younger and faster maturing cognacs that would become too woody if aged in Limousin wood.

Both woods are cut into planks which are allowed to dry slowly, exposed to the air and rain which naturally remove undesirable elements, make the tannins more palatable and create mould to develop the vanilla character in the lignins.

At 72% ABV, the spirit can leach considerable character from the wood. So the size and age of the cask is determined with care to control how much the spirit is exposed to the wood at any stage of its life. New wood is generally, but not always, reserved to hold younger brandies for a matter of months. Some brandies never see new oak at all while a few firms use new oak for up to four years.

Casks holding 350 litres are standard but some holding more can be found and the smaller the size of the cask, the greater the impact on the spirit. High strength alcohol may extract too much from the wood, so the spirit strength may be reduced to around 60% ABV before it's entered into the wood.

Historically, and primarily for ease of transportation, cognacs were aged in damp cellars on the banks of the river Charente, today most remain there, no longer for ease of transportation but because humidity reduces alcoholic strength faster than volume to the benefit of the cognac. Too dry a cellar and the liquid volume evaporates too quickly leaving less character and a spirit that is dry and hard. Depending on the nature of each barrel, thirty to fifty years may be necessary for the brandy to absorb all the tannin and lignin from the wood. But in time the wood becomes neutral and its only role is to permit continued oxidation.

Age does not guarantee quality but slowly the spirit oxidizes, extracting colour and character from the wood. Texture and depth concentrate through evaporation and the influence of oxygen seeping into the interior of the cask. After around twenty years some acquire an oily richness, described as *rancio* (a nutty character similar to sherry). This may remind some of cheese like Roquefort or of a rich fruit cake full of nuts and candied fruit. Such characteristics become increasingly intense over the years, transcending the flavours absorbed from the wood itself. Thus, the description *rancio* testifies to advanced levels of oxidation during long periods of maturation.

If still in cask after fifty years, the cognac is probably moved into special cellars called *paradis* (paradise) and stored there in wicker-encased glass jars to arrest further development.

During maturation, brandies from different regions and ages are constantly blended before being returned to cask until their final house styles are reached. VS (Very Special) can contain as many as forty cognacs, VSOP (Very Special Old Pale) as many as sixty and XO (Extra Old) as many as eighty cognacs.

Some cognac producers add a liquid called *boisé* to the casks. *Boisé* can be made by soaking wood chips in cognac or by boiling wood chips in water and then reducing the liquid. This process may take place over months or years. Its purpose is to accelerate the maturation process.

Before bottling, the cognac is gradually diluted to bottling strength, a delicate process that lasts several months because brandy and water do not mix easily. For this reason some producers use *petits eaux* (a mix of brandy and water, at a combined strength of around 15% ABV) to ease the process. Caramel may be added for consistent colour as well as sugar syrup for a sweeter, rounder taste, but these two additives are restricted to a maximum of 2%.

COGNAC CLASSIFICATIONS

Age classifications on cognac labels represent the youngest brandies in the blend. Most reputable producers age their brandies for longer than the statutory minimum.

All brandies are registered with the BNIC (Bureau National Interprofessionel du Cognac) the region's governing body and that body allocates *compte* (count) numbers to the brandies, as they age. It is important to note that the regulations relating to nomenclature and the compte system reflect minimum ages. Practice varies significantly among the cognac houses. A VSOP from one house could be older than an XO from another.

The *compte* system

- **Compte 00** covers the period from harvest to 31st March in the following year.

- **Compte 0** covers the period from 1st April following the harvest to 31st March in the following year.

- **Compte 2** is the minimum for XXX or VS, meaning the cognac has been aged for no less than two years.

- **Compte 4** is the minimum for VSOP, meaning at least four years but most will be aged from five to ten years, some, as many as fifteen years. The letters stand for Very Special Old Pale, a description of the pale brandies shipped to England in Victorian times and stored in dark cellars where evaporation was limited and less colour was absorbed from the wood.

- **Compte 6** is the minimum for any blend designated Napoleon, Extra, Vieux or Vieille Reserve although none of these terms are specifically defined. Actual ages and quality will vary significantly by brand. Compte 6 is also the minimum for XO, though this minimum age will rise to compte 10 by 2018.

- **Compte 10** is now the oldest designation to be controlled by the BNIC.

- **Vintage** has been recognized by the BNIC since 1988 to allow cognac to compete with armagnac brandies.

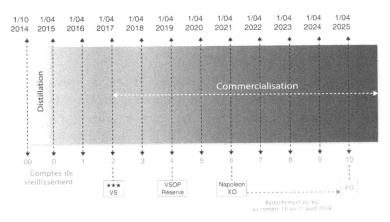

The compte system

ARMAGNAC

Armagnac is the generic name of France's oldest spirit. It celebrated its 700th anniversary in 2010. Vital Dufour was the Prior of Eauze in Armagnac from 1260 to 1327. He wrote an alphabetic and scientific encyclopaedia, dated 1310, that is now in the Vatican library in Rome. In one paragraph of this very useful book for conserving one's health and staying on top form, he outlines the virtues of *aygue ardente* (ardent waters), armagnac's ancestor:

This water, if taken medically and soberly is said to have forty virtues. It fries the egg, conserves meat cooked or crude, and in presence of herbs, extracts their virtues. It makes disappear redness and burning of the eyes, and stops tears from running; it cures hepatitis, cures gout, cankers and fistula by ingestion, restores the paralysed member by massage and heals wounds of the skin by application. It cures pain in the ears and deafness; it makes disappear stones in the kidneys and bladder and when anointed, it relieves headaches particularly those coming from a cold. It enlivens the spirit, partaken in moderation, recalls the past to memory, renders men joyous, preserves youth and retards senility. And when retained in the mouth, it loosens the tongue and emboldens the wit, if someone timid from time to time himself permits.

Armagnac is produced in the Armagnac region, a restricted and strictly controlled area south-east of Bordeaux in the Lot et Garonne, Gers and Landes departments in the heart of Gascony, a relatively unfamiliar region except to those who may recall d'Artagnan, the legendary character of Alexandre Dumas. The character was based upon Charles de Batz-Castelmore who left the Gers in 1646 to join the King's Company of Musketeers.

Prior to this time the area had been close to Al-Andalus, the Arabic name given to parts of the Iberian Peninsula and to a region just to the west, around Carcassonne and Béziers, which was governed by the Moors at various times from 711AD to 1492. Thanks to this close proximity to Islamic culture, the Gascons were among the first to benefit from the Arabs' knowledge of distilling, which helps to explain why armagnac was the first brandy to be distilled in France. (In 1387, it is told that Charles the Bad, King of Navarre, a region on the Atlantic coast that straddled the Pyrenees, died in agony when his sheets, soaked with the local eaux-de-vie, caught fire. Joan of Arc (1412–1431) was nicknamed 'The Armagnacaise'.) In 1461, regulations controlling sales at the market in Saint-Sever in Les Landes confirm that eaux-de-vie from the Armagnac area had been around for many years. Evidence exists that by the middle of the seventeenth century armagnac was being transported to Bordeaux and that the Dutch were including it in their shipments from that port. In the eighteenth century recognition grew for the superiority of certain armagnacs such as those from the Bas Armagnac region and this, doubtless, helped to grow exports. During the American War of Independence (1775–1783), the colonists chose armagnac in preference to cognac. In 1760, armagnac became the brandy of choice for King Louis XV and his court. By 1850, the Gers was the largest grape growing region in France until, in 1879, the phylloxera blight destroyed half of the vineyards.

Armagnac's lack of international recognition and its status as the poor relation to cognac have less to do with quality and more to do with location. Until railways and canals gave access to lucrative export markets, the region had no easy exit routes by sea or river. Maybe because of this, even today, there are as many as 800 producers of which 500 are independent and 300 are cooperatives. The brandies they make are true individuals and generally recognized to be less smoothed out by blending than cognacs. At their best, they are full of natural sweetness and rich in character. Their problem, historically, has been that many have been sold when still too young and unbalanced.

As with cognac, the terroir is key to armagnac. Here, however, rather than the chalk that is so important in cognac, the soil consists of clay and sand left by the departing water to the west as well as clay and chalk to the east. Armagnacs from the sandy soils traditionally display great finesse and class. But armagnac's individual and varied character depends as much on climate, grapes, the manner of distillation, the wood choice and length of maturation as on the soil.

Unlike in Cognac, brandy here can account for a low share of any property's overall production because many of the winegrowers produce good quality table wines able to deliver healthy and reliable annual returns. Total production amounts to scarcely 4% of that of cognac, but more than 40% is exported.

At its best, armagnac can offer a deep natural sweetness and a rich complexity unmatched by any other brandy. According to Salvatore Calabrese, 'The difference between cognac and armagnac is to imagine a length of velvet and another of silk and to stroke them. The velvet has a deep rich texture and that is armagnac. The silk is pure finesse and that is cognac.'

Armagnac climate

The region, protected by the Landes forest to the west and the Pyrenees in the south, enjoys a temperate climate, influenced predominantly by two maritime systems. Cool, moist, temperate weather flows from the Atlantic in the west and warmer air flows up from the Mediterranean in the south. Occasionally the two systems collide, resulting in potentially disastrous storms. But usually the area enjoys a steady climate, warmer and sunnier than in Cognac. Winters can be harsh. Summers are hot and humid with dewy mornings that encourage thicker grape skins and, therefore, more flavour. Also, unlike in Cognac, the climate here ensures full maturation of the grapes, leading to rich and flavourful brandies. In Bas Armagnac to the west and closer to the Atlantic Ocean and in Haut Armagnac to the east of the appellation, there is greater rainfall than in the Ténarèze.

Armagnac regions

Post-phylloxera, on 25th May 1909, the Fallières Decree was signed outlining the appellation and delimiting the three areas of production: Haut Armagnac, Ténarèze and Bas Armagnac. In 1936, the armagnac appellation was declared. Since then the authorities have significantly reduced the area of the appellation, virtually eliminating the Haut Armagnac region from the appellation.

Today, across the whole region, less than 4,000 hectares are planted with vines for the production of armagnac. The vast majority of the region's vines produce grapes for dry white wine.

Armagnac region

Bas Armagnac accounts for around two thirds of the vineyards that produce armagnac, stretching to dunes in the west, covered in a heavy top soil, known as *boulbène*, and rich in marine sediment over sand. In some areas this is mixed with iron, giving rise to the designation, *sables fauves* (tawny sands), while in others, to the north-west, the soil becomes more predominantly clay. The acidic soil drains rapidly, providing potential for great quality and fruity, yet light and delicate, brandies.

Ténarèze accounts for less than one third of vineyards producing armagnac. The soil is a rich mix of *boulbène* over clay and chalk. The climate tends to be drier and warmer. The brandies are more floral and fruity in style but rich and full-bodied. They are likely to benefit from at least ten years ageing, if not more.

Haut Armagnac rises to the east. Only small pockets of sand exist here in a predominantly limestone area. Brandy production is small, confined to a mere forty-two hectares.

Armagnacs that carry any of the above regional designations on the label must contain spirit made only from grapes grown and distilled in that region. The simple description 'armagnac' permits a blend of brandies from the three regions.

Armagnac grapes

Owing to a warmer climate, grapes ripen earlier here than in the Cognac region and produce wines of around 9% ABV, but they are still fairly acidic. Unlike in Cognac, ten varieties of white grapes are permitted. Before the phylloxera blight the main grape was what is now called the Folle Blanche. But when the bug was eradicated many producers replaced this grape with varieties less susceptible to disease, including Ugni Blanc and Colombard. Later a hybrid, Baco 22A, was introduced. Today these four are the usual choice. The other grape varieties permitted in the region include: Plante de Graisse (certain producers are currently experimenting with this variety), Meslier St François, Clairette de Gascogne, Jurançon Blanc, Mauzac Blanc and Mauzac Rosé. Ugni Blanc accounts for more than half of all vines in the region, delivering a high yield, low alcohol and neutral flavoured acidic wine. The grape is not as powerful as Baco 22A and is less aromatic than Folle Blanche but it combines well with the wood. Folle Blanche was the choice variety before the phylloxera blight but in the 1870s it proved to be susceptible to grey rot. It now accounts for 8% of plantings and produces wines low in alcohol and high in acidity, delicate in character but full of floral aromatics. The grape's introduction into a blend can contribute lots of finesse and its use in armagnac blanche (see below) can be particularly attractive.

Baco 22A was introduced in the late 1930s by a M Baco. It is a hybrid obtained from the Folle Blanche and an American grape called Noah. The result retains some of the Folle Blanche's aromatics but the grape is much tougher. It accounts for 40% of plantings and is the only hybrid grape afforded appellation status in France. It delivers full-bodied, fat, almost oily brandies, lacking finesse but full of the scents of ripe fruit. With significant age, these deliver armagnac's distinctive and rich aromas of prunes and ripe fruit. It is a robust grape variety needing very little chemical treatment.

Colombard is a popular grape for fragrant, dry table wines or Floc de Gascogne (see below) but little is used for armagnac. It accounts for 2% of plantings. This grape is rarely a success on its own but its spicy aromas can be an excellent addition to armagnac blends.

Fermentation is usually natural with yeasts coming from the grape skins. The wine may be left on the lees but not for long because no sulphites or any other additives can be used to protect it. If such additives were used, distillation would concentrate them as well as the wine character.

Armagnac distillation

Early distillation of armagnac was conducted twice in pot stills but the process was labour-intensive and costly. In the early nineteenth century, Edouard Adam experimented with various forms of continuous distillation and in 1818 he registered a patent for a process which local distillers modified to become what we know today as the alambic armagnacais. The oldest version, which was bought in 1804 and remains in use today at Domaine d'Ognoas, was the product of one of Adam's experiments.

The alambic armagnacais is a small continuous column still to which wheels are added so, regardless of size, farmers could have their wines distilled before the threat of oxidation and without great cost. Today 90% of farmers use this mobile still and 95% of armagnac is distilled in the alambic armagnacais: wood is used to heat 25% and gas to heat the remaining 75%. The armagnac column is still very small and permits lots of heavy congeners and vapours rich in fusel oils, to pass over into the condenser. The size of this still, the relatively low heat generated in it and the traditional number of only five plates placed in the column result in a spirit below 60% ABV and often nearer 50% ABV, rich in texture, very aromatic and full of impurities, or what those in the area prefer to call flavours. All spirit must exit the still between 52% and 72.4% ABV, although most range from 52% to 60% ABV. Actual strength depends on the number of plates inserted into the still.

Mobile alambic armagnacais

The lower the ABV percentage off the still, the greater the level of congeners in the spirit and so the greater the need for maturation in wood. At 52% ABV, the distillate contains twice as many congeners as at 60% ABV. A typical spirit drawn from the armagnacais still contains a little more than 50% pure alcohol and just under 50% water. The difference, around 4%, consists of the flavour-giving compounds of esters, acids and congeners. This 4% compares with nearer 2.5% in cognac, 1.5% in whisky and less than 1% in vodka and can be a reason for armagnac being raw and unpalatable without many years of maturation in wood.

This process is costly and full of risk. So, today, few grape growers in the area rely on armagnac alone. Instead, many of the generally small and family-run farms rely more on cattle or other animals or cereals or they produce wine. However, in time, these same compounds oxidize and transform into the aromatic complexity and rich, palate-coating texture so typical of traditional armagnac.

What distinguishes armagnac from other brandies is that the wine, drawn from the tank on top of the condensing column, heats as it drops through the perforated plates towards the boiler, turns into steam and evaporates. The vapours rise back up through tubes in the plates where they are forced into contact with the incoming wine. The vapours become saturated and highly charged with the wine's fragrance and fruit. They continue to rise before exiting the top of the still, passing over into the adjacent column and flowing through the cold condensing coil to drop as liquid into a barrel. The alambic armagnacais is not able to reach high temperatures so the low alcohol distillate retains many of the esters, acids and congeners that double distillation in a pot still eliminates. Heads are retained for their aromatic qualities unless the wine quality is not good. Tails are less palatable and so they remain, circulating in the system until removed by the distiller. In a pot still the heads and tails exit the still for recycling.

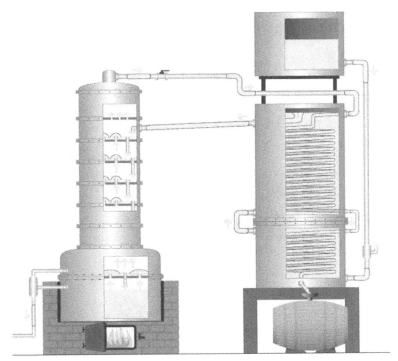

Armagnac condenser

The pot still was banned from 1943 to 1971 when only the single continuous still was authorized. But the pot was authorized again in

1972. Both remain permitted today. Some producers now use the
pot still to distil a spirit nearer 70% ABV, a higher level of alcohol
than is achieved in the traditional armagnac column. The resulting
distillate contains fewer impurities and is more suitable for bottling
or blending at a relatively young age.

Distillation must finish no later than 31st March of the year
following harvest, unless brought forward by annual decree. In
practice, most finish distillation by the end of January. No sulphur
or added sugar is permitted.

Wood-fired alembic

Armagnac maturation

The armagnac distillate is generally placed in new 400-litre oak casks, called *pièces*, for between six months and two years before being transferred into older barrels for further maturation. Annual transfer from one barrel to another helps to aerate the spirit and to accelerate maturation. Great armagnac needs to age for a considerable time in wood and the greater the quantity of congeners, the longer the time required for maturation. However, since the re-introduction of double pot distillation, which produces fewer congeners, a few producers now use only pot distilled armagnacs or blend armagnacs from pot and continuous stills to create brandies ready for earlier bottling.

Some producers may not know the source of their wood because, for them, the quality of grain within any wood is more important than the forest it comes from. Some will say the toasting process can reduce differences between the woods anyway. Nevertheless, different woods are used. Traditionally, the oak used was *pédoncule*, or black oak from the Monlezun forest. Now Limousin accounts for around 85% of barrels. The wood has a similar open grain, allowing plenty of colour and flavour to be extracted. Tronçais and sessile oak are tight grained and less forthcoming, yielding less colour. They are also more expensive and thus a rare choice. Some producers choose their own oaks from the Monlezun forest and use their own coopers to cut and dry the staves. Some have replanted forests with local oak to benefit future generations.

The wood is always air-dried for three to six years to deplete the astringent bitters and tannins as well as to season it. Though the cost may be too great for some, (at least €700 per barrel), new wood is usually the first choice to encourage initial transfer of lots of colour, vanilla and spice. Afterwards, progressively older barrels are used to reduce the impact of the oak and to compensate for the physical differences of each barrel. In later years, even in the more neutral casks, slow oxidation continues.

The level of alcohol slowly drops while the brandy softens and becomes more viscous. Dry conditions tend to lead to a slower reduction in alcohol and a more rapid loss of liquid. More humid cellars encourage a more rapid reduction in alcohol.

Armagnacs are 'worked' throughout their maturation, meaning they are pumped out of their barrels at least once a year, aerated in tanks and then returned to their casks. Topping up the levels in casks to keep them full and reduce evaporation to a minimum is common. If the armagnac is to be sold as 'vintage', only the vintage year's armagnac may be used.

Water may be introduced to reduce alcoholic strength, but this is best done gradually over many years. Spirits distilled to low levels of alcohol do not lend themselves so well to reduction and many are allowed to reduce naturally in the barrel for bottling at the strength they finally exit from the wood, generally between 40% and 48% ABV. This is a slow, costly and potentially risky business.

Unlike with cognac, armagnac is blended for bottling and not during maturation, allowing distillers to bottle vintages. Also, most producers age each grape variety separately and only blend later on, usually around six months before bottling. Although armagnac matures more slowly than cognac and the compte system applies, regulations permit armagnac to be sold younger than cognac.

Legally, up to 2% of an armagnac's content can be sugar syrup though few producers add sugar.

Armagnac classifications

These minimum ages represent the youngest brandies in the blend:

- **VS** must be minimum compte 1 or twelve months old from 31st March following the harvest. Most are aged for at least three years.

- **VSOP** must be minimum compte 4 or four years old but usually the youngest is aged closer to seven years.

- **Napoleon** must be at least six years old and can carry an actual age statement if preferred.

- **XO** must be at least six years old but nearer to ten years is more likely. XO can carry an actual age statement if preferred.

- **Hors d'Age** must be aged at least ten years.

- **Vintage** must be aged at least ten years and can be described as XO, if preferred.

To ensure the provenance of vintage armagnacs and those carrying age statements, the BNIA, armagnac's governing body, must be informed of any movements whether in bulk, in bottle or on paper.

ARMAGNAC BLANCHE

In 2005, armagnac blanche became the youngest French appellation in the world of spirits. The selected grapes are Folle Blanche, Ugni Blanc and Baco, used pure or blended, but Folle Blanche dominates as its fruity aromatics are key to the brandy's charm. Distillation is early to preserve the wines' quality and to a higher level of alcohol than for armagnac. The distillate is stored in inert containers for a minimum of three months and often longer for aeration to enhance the aromatics and to mellow the distillate. Blanche is rich and elegant, strong and rounded and, as such, is ideal for enjoyment as an aromatic aperitif, in a cocktail, or as a gourmet accompaniment to smoked fish, cold meats or to enhance numerous desserts.

FLOC DE GASCOGNE

This is three parts unfermented grape juice, from the Armagnac area, fortified with one part armagnac, which is aged for one year but not usually in wood. Both white and red (legally referred to as 'rosé') are bottled at between 16% and 18% ABV and drunk locally as aperitifs. It has enjoyed appellation status since 1990. *Floc* means 'bunch of flowers' in the local patois.

FRENCH GRAPE BRANDY

Defined as a wine-based spirit, this is a blend of highly rectified grape spirit from non-AOC vineyards, aged in oak for varying times. It can be blended with other brandies distilled from fermented grape juice or from crushed but not pressed grape pulp and skin. Most colour results from the addition of caramel and, despite designations like 'Napoleon' or 'XXXXX' on many labels, the brandy offers little of the complexity and other rewards these meaningless descriptors might suggest.

SPANISH BRANDY: BRANDY DE JEREZ AND BRANDY DEL PENÈDES

The Moors ruled southern Spain from the eighth century for over 700 years. They brought their knowledge of distilling and their stills to Spain. Initially, the brandy they distilled was used locally and only for medicines or to fortify local wines. The first record of maturing distilled wine here dates from 1580. By the seventeenth century, the Dutch were shipping this brandy around the world and the term, 'holandas', still used to describe the best, provides continuing evidence of this early influence.

Though called brandy de Jerez, the Palomino grapes grown around Jerez on Andalucia's chalky soil are very rarely used. Instead, the white Airen grape grown in La Mancha in central Spain is the usual choice. La Mancha's hot climate ensures these grapes are full of sugar, able to deliver wines high in alcohol, at 11%–13% ABV. When distilled, the alcohol and flavours in this wine are less concentrated than in the case of the wines distilled for cognac. The resulting spirit is never very complex but always full-bodied, lush and sweet. Brandy de Jerez was awarded denominaciónes de origen (DO) status in 1989.

The wines distilled in La Mancha are classified into three styles:

- **Holandas** is the best quality. It must be double distilled in pot stills (*alquitaras*) and the distillate must exit below 70% ABV to retain more congeners and character. A *solera gran reserva* usually contains 100% holandas.

- **Aguardiente** is single distilled in a column still. The distillate must exit below 85% ABV. A *solera* is usually a blend of aguardiente and aguardiente destilado. Frequent transfers between barrels take place to accelerate oxidation.

- **Aguardiente destilado** is single distilled in a column still and exits from 86% to 94.5% ABV. The stronger the spirit, the less flavour it has, meaning aguardiente destilado is not used in the best quality brandies. When it is used, the law dictates that aguardiente destilado must account for less than 50% of a blend.

After distillation, the brandy must be shipped to the southwest corner of Spain to mature in and around Jerez, El Puerto de Santa María,and Sanlúcar de Barrameda. Here, the new spirit is entered into a solera system which is a series of large, ex-sherry casks, called butts. The casks must have held sherry for at least three years and should hold between 250 and 600 litres. Some spirit may first spend a short period of 'static ageing' before entering the solera system. The solera system itself consists of rows of casks, stacked on top of one another so that the brandy can transfer down from one to the other. Each lower cask holds a slightly older spirit than the one above. When the brandy is drawn off (racked) from the final butt on the ground it is replenished with brandy drawn from the butt above and the process is repeated up the solera to the top row of butts, where the newly distilled brandy fills the space. No more than a third of the volume may be removed for bottling in any year. This process blends together a variety of vintages and results in considerable oxidation. Both the blending and the oxidation help to accelerate maturation.

Solera designations

- **Solera** is the designation used for the youngest style of Spanish brandy. It always contains the highest percentage of column distillate and the 'dynamic' maturation can last as little as six months.

- **Solera reserva** is aged for at least one year and is normally a blend of column and pot distillates.

- **Solera gran reserva** is aged a minimum of three years but the best are frequently aged for twelve to fifteen years and are almost always made exclusively from pot distillate. Additives like prune juice and other fruit or nut extracts are permitted to enhance the sweet and fruity notes. To ensure minimum qualities, the level of congeners must be 150 mg per litre in solera, 200 mg per litre in solera reserva and in excess of 250 mg per litre in solera gran reserva. The overall objective is to create richness and softness in the finished brandy and to deliver brandies that are notably less austere than others, thus ideal for mixing. A key factor in the style of any individual brandy is the nature of the sherry previously stored in the cask, for example, the use of ex-oloroso casks results in especially rich brandies.

In the north-east corner of Spain, brandies from Penedès, a region of Catalonia, near Barcelona, are much closer to cognac in both their geography and style. They are distilled in pots, some are aged in a solera system while others are not, but Limousin oak is used. The brandy is neither as rich nor as sweet as brandy de Jerez nor as elegant as cognac.

POMACE BRANDIES AND MARC

France and Italy are the largest producers of pomace brandies. Both are made from the lees or solid matter (pomace) of grape pulp, skins and stems remaining after the grapes have been crushed and pressed to extract the juice for wine. EU regulations state that marc spirit, grape marc and grappa are spirit drinks produced from grape pomace that is fermented and distilled either directly by water vapour or after water has been added. Distillation must be carried out in the presence of the pomace to less than 86% ABV.

Grappa's origins are unclear but this generic Italian term originates from the town Bassano del Grappa where Bartolo Nardini first distilled wines towards the end of the eighteenth century. Grappa's spiritual home remains northern Italy, where the climate ensures good acidity in the wines and where vintners, wanting to waste nothing from their grapes, have traditionally added water to the pomace and distilled this to create an aromatic spirit that is usually enjoyed with coffee.

They can be rather raw in character, although some may be rested for a while in old wood to mellow, while others will be stored in glass containers ready for sale in the following spring. Their minimal age and rare contact with wood means these brandies retain lots of fresh and fruity aromas from the grapes.

Italy produces a substantial amount of grappa, some on an industrial scale while others are more artisanal. Initial quality was generally poor, but in 1970 the EEC decreed that a tenth of the community's grape juice should be distilled. This, combined with moves in Italy to improve wine-making, resulted in more and better quality juice remaining in the pomace. Efforts were also made to distil the pomace within twenty-four hours of pressing, after the stalks and stems had been removed but while it was still moist. The result is that even mass-produced grappa can now be perfectly palatable.

Basic grappa is made from a blend of grapes. But the increasing popularity of varietal wines has encouraged greater production of single varietal grappa (grappa di vitigno). Top artisanal grappa is always distilled from the residue of the first pressing of a single grape variety. White grapes tend to yield grappa with more flavour: aromatic with floral overtones, intensely fruity and delicate, and very reminiscent of their source grapes. Some grappa is distilled from grapes grown only in the region specified on the label. Distillati d'uva is distilled from whole grapes resulting in fuller, usually sweeter flavours and more aromatics.

Grappa can be classified as *invecchiata* (aged), *stravecchia* (very old) and *riserva* (reserve). The letters UTF on the label mean the distiller is the producer.

French marc is generally consumed locally and often adopts the name of its local wine production area, such as the relatively rich and full-bodied marc de Bourgogne, the aromatic marc de Champagne and the single varietal marc d'Alsace. *Vieux* indicates that it was aged a minimum of three years; *très vieux* a minimum of six years; and *hors d'âge* a minimum of ten years.

Marc de Gewurztraminer from Alsace is particularly noteworthy because it retains much of the distinctive perfumed nose and spicy character of the grape. These are pot distilled to around 70% ABV. The best are aged five to ten years in oak barrels that were previously used for wine.

California produces pomace brandies broadly in the Italian style. They are usually called grappa, even when they are made from non-Italian grape varieties. This is also true of the pomace brandies produced in Canada.

ITALIAN BRANDIES

Italian brandy production dates back to at least the sixteenth century but there are no official brandy producing regions and the category didn't even officially exist until 1948 when regulations banned use of the word 'conac' on labels. Most of these are distilled in column stills, though small artisanal producers sometimes use pots. The two grades, standard and de luxe, can be sold after two years in wood but most standards remain in wood for around six years and de luxe for ten. Descriptions like *vecchia* (old) have no legal definition. Italian brandies tend to be light and delicate with hints of residual sugars.

GERMAN BRANDIES

German monks were distilling brandy by the fourteenth century and distillers organized their own guild by 1588, yet German brandies have no real heritage or roots. Historically, they were labeled as cognac but, after that term was forbidden, the description, 'weinbrand' was coined in 1907 and registered by Hugo Asbach.

Despite Germany's production of acid white grapes none are used for making brandy, instead, German brandies are made from imported grapes, usually from the hot south such as from Italy and southern France, though some are from the Cognac and Armagnac regions. Most of the grapes used are high in sugar and low in acidity, meaning they produce rather fat spirits. They are distilled in pot and column stills and contain flavourings such as caramel, *boisé* and prune juice.

The usual age is at least six months, but the designation *uralt* (age-old) signifies an age of at least one year, first in small new casks and then in larger casks.

The character of all German brandies tends to be warm, sweetish and bland. They are best enjoyed as the base for mixers.

CALIFORNIA BRANDIES

Brandy production in California dates back to the Spanish missions in the eighteenth and nineteenth centuries so California makes brandy in the Spanish style, though it is lighter and best used for mixing.

Californian table grape varieties are used together with the classic European varieties. The spirit must be distilled below 85% ABV. Most are distilled in huge stainless steel continuous stills, resulting in light-bodied brandies. However, some may use pot-still brandy to add extra weight.

The minimum age is two years though at least four are more usual and some may age even longer. Maturation is usually in ex-bourbon barrels to add richness to the brandy though some, and particularly the pot distillers, use French oak. Some producers use the solera system to age their brandies.

Up to 2.5% of additives such as fruits, caramel, sugars or fortified wines are allowed.

MEXICAN BRANDIES

In Mexico most wine is distilled into brandy. Spanish conquistador Hernán Cortés seeded the brandy culture by requiring all incoming ships to bring vines to Mexico. Usually distilled in continuous stills, but also in pot stills, from a mix of grape varieties, the brandies are generally aged in solera systems. Mexican brandy is very much in the Spanish style: light, clean, sweet and best drunk long with mixers.

PISCO

South American brandies are generally confined to their domestic markets but pisco is one that is better known in export markets. Pisco is a grape brandy, distilled in pots from freshly fermented grape juice, clear or lightly coloured, with a perfumed fragrance. Possible origins of the name include an old Quechua Indian word *pisccu*, meaning 'flying bird', suggestive of the spirit's powerful effects, 'Piskus' who were local Indian settlers and Pisco, the port city at the mouth of the river of the same name. From here the spirit was initially exported with the name 'Pisco' written on the containers to indicate its origin. Both Chile and Peru have rights to use the name.

When the Spanish defeated the Incas in the 1530s, they introduced vines and set up a vice-royalty that stretched from the Caribbean to what is now southern Chile. At that time the countries we know today as Chile and Peru did not exist. As late as the nineteenth century, brandies produced in what we now recognize as the separate countries of Bolivia, Chile and Peru could have all been shipped out of the port of Pisco, now situated in Peru.

In Peru, pisco classification is based on only using specified grape varietals, Quebrante, Mollar and Negre Corriente which are classified as non-aromatic; Italia which is a table wine grape; plus Moscatel, Torontel and Albilla which are classified as aromatic. These generate four grape-based Peruvian styles of pisco: puro non-aromatico (Peru's most popular style) and puro aromatico, both distilled from one single grape; pisco acholado, a blend; and mosto verde, a speciality made only in great vintage years and distilled from partially fermented must. Production is restricted to five regions, which differ in terms of soil and climate.

It is usual to choose wines only from the first pressing for production of pisco. Fermentation is long with no added sugars and using only natural yeasts. Only single distillation is permitted, to bottle strength, and the distillate must be rested for three months, although most will age for up to one year in ceramic, plastic or stainless steel.

In Chile, on 16 May 1931, a government decree awarded the name pisco to all those brandies produced in what are now known as the Atacama and Coquimbo regions, between the 27th and 32nd parallels. This is a predominantly sub-desert climate with unusual characteristics due to the influence of the Pacific anti-cyclone, minimal cloud cover and no rainfall for nine to ten months of the year. As in Peru, grapes are grown on the coastal plains and in the valleys that sweep down from the Andes to the sea.

Regulations dating from the nineteenth century gradually formalized what had become traditional habits until a law in 1916 defined natural pisco as genuinely pure, produced directly from a special grape with no aromatic additives or other substances, bottled directly by the distiller.

The best come from microclimates in the Elqui valley. It is very hot here during the day but the temperatures drop sharply at night, allowing grapes to retain their acidity. There are four other designated areas, the Copiapó, Huasco, Choapa and Limarí valleys.

Chilean law now establishes which grapes are permitted. They are the aromatic grapes, often clones of the Muscat, though other aromatic grapes are used occasionally. The permitted varieties are: Cassellas Mosque Vrai, Yellow Muscat, Early White Muscat, Muscat of Alexandria, Muscat of Austria, Muscat Frontignan, Muscat Hamburg, Black Muscat, Pink or Pastilla Muscat, Muscat Canelli, Muscat Orange, Pedro Jimenez and Torontel.

The grapes are first pressed and the juice, or *mosto*, is chilled slightly to preserve aromatics before four to five days of natural fermentation on the skins, again, to capture maximum aromatics. The part-fermented wine is then removed from the solids and transferred to holding tanks to complete fermentation after around thirty days. Distillation to around 60%–63% ABV completes the grape juice's transformation into pisco. Chilean pisco can be diluted to bottling strength and aged for just a few months or for as many as two years in American oak or native beech before it is bottled and labeled, according to four classifications.

- **Corriente** or **tradicional** is the basic style, usually unaged and kept in stainless steel tanks for a limited time. It is colourless and bottled at 30%–35% ABV.

- **Especial** is aged for a short time and bottled at 35%–40% ABV.

- **Reservado** is aged longer and bottled at 40% ABV.

- **Gran pisco** is aged for the longest period of time and bottled at 43% ABV. Maturation is usually executed in large used barrels that give the spirit a pink/lemony hue.

In Bolivia, pisco is called Singani. It is made from the Moscatel grape and has floral aromas similar to Chilean pisco.

SOUTH AFRICAN BRANDIES

Brandy was distilled by the original Dutch settlers from 1672, twenty years after the colony's founding. It was generally poor in taste until a Frenchman named René Santhagens improved production standards towards the end of the nineteenth century. South Africa is the only country in the world where brandy is the dominant spirit. The majority of drinkers come from the black community, as in America.

Distilled in pot and column stills from Colombard, Chenin, Folle Blanche and local grapes, this brandy is mostly light in flavour and good for mixing though a number of top quality pot-still brandies can be found.

AUSTRALIAN BRANDIES

Early settlers distilled brandy to make port. Now distilled in South Australia, Victoria and New South Wales, in pot and continuous stills, the new spirit exits the still between 74% and 83% ABV.

Ageing is from two to twenty years but the 'old' designation usually means a minimum of five; 'very old' indicates a minimum of ten years.

Quiz on brandies

1. The town of Cognac lies on the banks of which river?

   A. Seine
   B. Garonne
   C. Charente
   D. Dordogne

2. In 1549, which was the first nation to ship wines from the Cognac region?

   A. England
   B. France
   C. Spain
   D. Holland

3. Which characteristic of grapes grown in the Cognac region makes them ideal for distillation?

   A. Acidity
   B. Sweetness
   C. Fruitiness
   D. Level of alcohol

4. From which country did Richard Hennessy travel to France in 1765?

   A. Ireland
   B. England
   C. Scotland
   D. Wales

5. From which country did Thomas Hine travel to France in 1791?

   A. Ireland
   B. England
   C. Scotland
   D. Wales

6. In which decade did the phylloxera aphid blight destroy the cognac vines?

   A. 1850s
   B. 1860s
   C. 1870s
   D. 1880s

7. The Cognac region is divided into how many classified areas?

   A. Four
   B. Six
   C. Eight
   D. Ten

8. In Fine Champagne what percentage of the wine must come from the Grande Champagne area?

   A. 25%
   B. 40%
   C. 50%
   D. 55%

9. Which is the smallest classified area in the Cognac region?

   A. Borderies
   B. Fins Bois
   C. Grande Champagne
   D. Petite Champagne

10. Which of the classified areas provides the bulk of cognac?

   A. Bons Bois
   B. Fins Bois
   C. Bois Ordinaires
   D. Petite Champagne

11. Which is the dominant grape used for cognac, accounting for 98% of production?

   A. Colombard
   B. Folle Blanche
   C. Semillon
   D. Ugni Blanc

12. By law, wines for cognac must be distilled by the end of which month, following the harvest?

    A. March
    B. December
    C. June
    D. No rules

13. For cognac what is the maximum level of alcohol permitted when the spirit exits the second still?

    A. 55% ABV
    B. 84% ABV
    C. 65% ABV
    D. 72% ABV

14. What is the minimum age in wood for the cognac classification VSOP?

    A. Three years
    B. Four years
    C. Five years
    D. Six years

15. Which of these is classified as a pomace brandy?

    A. Pisco
    B. Grappa
    C. Calvados
    D. Armagnac

16. France's oldest brandy comes from what region?

    A. Charente
    B. Normandy
    C. Gascony
    D. Loire

17. Which of these areas accounts for the largest share of armagnac vineyards?

    A. Haut Armagnac
    B. Ténarèze
    C. Bas Armagnac
    D. Les Landes

18. Which of these grapes is renowned for its floral aromatics and is a popular choice for armagnac blanche?

    A. Baco 22A
    B. Ugni Blanc
    C. Colombard
    D. Folle Blanche

19. Spirit usually exits the alambic armagnacais in what range of alcoholic strengths?

    A. 52%–60% ABV
    B. 55%–65% ABV
    C. 60%–68% ABV
    D. 65%–72% ABV

20. Armagnac blanche became the youngest French appellation in what year?

    A. 1871
    B. 1932
    C. 1976
    D. 2005

21. French grape brandy, classified as Napoleon, must be aged a minimum of how many years?

    A. Two years
    B. Four years
    C. Eight years
    D. No minimum

22. The Airen grape used in production of Spanish brandy is grown where?

A. Penedès
B. La Mancha
C. Jerez
D. Sanlucar de Barameda

23. What is the term used to describe the best quality Spanish brandy?

A. Aguardiente
B. Aguardients destilado
C. Holandas
D. Destilado

24. Spanish brandy classified as 'solera reserva' must have been aged at least how many years?

A. One year
B. Two years
C. Three years
D. Four years

25. Which of these terms is used to describe basic Chilean pisco that's usually not been aged?

A. Especial
B. Corriente
C. Gran Pisco
D. Reservado

MAKING COCKTAILS WITH BRANDY

Brandy is underrepresented in cocktails of the past, probably due to the fact that, of all the major categories, brandy's occasions for drinking and the rituals that surround its service are the most cemented. This is a crying shame as grape brandies and ones made from other fruits are some of the most mixable of spirits. They combine well with both citrus and soft fruits as well as working with more complex spirituous ingredients.

Pisco Sour

There are few cocktails that define a spirit like the Pisco Sour. Hugely popular in the pisco-producing countries of Chile and Peru, its reach has expanded thanks to stories from returning holidaymakers and the new breed of restaurateurs introducing authentic South American food around the globe.

Although aged versions of pisco are available, the vast majority are simply rested in steel or glass and therefore lend themselves to recipes involving citrus juice or, specifically, lime and lemon juice. If you can find ripe South American limes then these can be used on their own but the drink will often benefit from the inclusion of lemon juice to help reduce the astringency.

Like many drinks that are popular across whole continents there are numerous ways of combining the ingredients and variations in the recipe. I have tasted blended versions as well as shaken drinks served over cubed and crushed ice but my favourite is served straight up.

50ml pisco
12.5ml lemon juice
12.5ml lime juice
20ml simple syrup (see page 95)
½ white of an egg
6 drops Amargo Chuncho bitters

Add all the ingredients apart from the bitters into a cocktail shaker and shake hard without ice for twenty seconds. This 'dry shake' will incorporate large amounts of air into the mixture, creating a considerable quantity of egg white-based foam. Open the shaker, fill with ice and shake again as normal. Strain into a chilled, small wine glass or a stemmed sour glass and delicately place the drops of the Amargo Chuncho bitters on to the top of the foam. This is often easier if a small straw or pipette is used, as it is difficult to be accurate with the bitters bottle itself. Amargo Chuncho is widely available but Angostura bitters make an acceptable substitute.

Sidecar

The Sidecar cocktail was created around the end of the First World War, with The Ritz hotel in Paris having a strong claim to its invention. Named after the motorcycle and sidecar combination used by a dashing American army reconnaissance captain, it is a blend of two of France's most wonderful spirits, cognac and Cointreau, a strong liqueur flavoured with both sweet and bitter oranges. The drink is balanced with fresh lemon, and much of the discussion about the recipe stems from the proportions of the three ingredients. Originally calling for equal parts of the three ingredients, it quickly mutated into a drink with two parts cognac to one part each of lemon juice and Cointreau. Both recipes have equal amounts of lemon and liqueur, but as Cointreau is less sweet than many liqueurs this can lead to a slightly sour drink. To balance this the Sidecar is often served in a glass with a sugared rim to bring extra sweetness on the lips while maintaining the drink's dry finish.

40ml cognac
20ml Cointreau
20ml lemon juice

To produce a sugar rim, sparingly wet the rim of the cocktail glass with lemon juice and sprinkle on caster sugar. Wipe away any excess and place the glass in the freezer. This will allow the sugar to set slightly. Place all the ingredients in a cocktail shaker and shake. Strain into the pre-rimmed glass and serve.

When making this drink for guests it can be a nice ritual to up the quantities of all ingredients slightly and serve the excess in a small shot glass on the side, literally the sidecar.

Choosing a cognac with which to make this and other cocktails can often be a decision made with the wallet. The drink works well with both sweet, dark styles and lighter, drier styles of brandy and the simple nature of the recipe means that higher quality expressions will not be lost. I recommend using at least a VSOP cognac but Sidecars made from finer cognacs are a wonderful treat.

Big Appleberry

Nearly eighty per cent of modern cocktail recipes are based on a sweet and sour balance, using a liqueur or syrup and corresponding quantities of lemon or lime juice. Occasionally, however, a recipe is created that conforms to that idea of balance but doesn't require citrus ingredients. The Big Appleberry is one such drink. Cognac is famed for both its structure and finesse and sometimes the addition of lemon juice could be thought to mask some of these nuances. So this drink uses fruit to provide small amounts of free sugars and acid while still allowing the cognac to express itself fully. Sweet grapes and tart raspberries, blackberries and redcurrants produce a backdrop for the brandy to create an amazing long drink.

60ml cognac
5 red grapes
5 raspberries
5 blackberries
1 truss redcurrants
80ml pressed apple juice

Reserve a few pretty fruits for a garnish and then crush the rest thoroughly in a cocktail tin (to avoid the potential for injury using the glass half of the shaker for this task is not recommended) before adding the other ingredients. Strain into a tall 14oz sling or highball glass and garnish with the reserved fruits.

This drink, like all drinks using fresh fruits, works best when the fruits are in season. To be sure, taste the fruit beforehand. If the berries and currants are particularly tart a dash of simple syrup can be added to the recipe. Flash-frozen fruits are a good alternative, as it doesn't matter if the fruits lose their texture. They will be broken down in the shaker anyway.

Although lighter styles will be more than acceptable, the Big Appleberry works best with a big cognac. Colour alone is not a foolproof guide to weight or style because manufacturers can add caramel to achieve a colour consistent with their house style but a weighty cognac, typically deep red-brown in colour through age, will be ideal for this drink. This cocktail also works well with armagnac and aged Spanish and Greek brandies.

10

LIQUEURS

BACKGROUND TO LIQUEURS

The initial purpose of liqueurs, or cordials as they're called in America was to capture and make palatable the medicinal benefits of herbs, fruits, spices and plants. Early knowledge of how to produce them was vested in the learned few, usually monks, until the arrival of exotic ingredients from distant lands and broader knowledge of distillation encouraged commercial production in Europe.

In time, some regions became recognized for the use of local or imported ingredients and/or skill in making certain liqueurs. In mountain areas, for example, plants and herbs were readily available for compounding and distillation. The abundance and quality of local fruits offered many countries and regions opportunities to distil local specialities like crème de cassis, distilled from the blackcurrants that grew around Dijon. Imported fruits prompted production of exotic liqueurs in ports, such as curaçao in Amsterdam. The first record of commercial production of liqueurs was in 1575, when the Bols family opened het Lootsje and began to distil liqueurs just outside the walls of Amsterdam. Lucas Bols was born in 1652; he was a major shareholder in the VOC, the Dutch East India Company, and he used the exotic herbs, spices and fruits shipped back to Holland by the company to greatly expand the Bols range of liqueurs.

Though the purpose of a liqueur was initially medicinal, increasingly, its intricate blend of flavours, aromatics, sugars and alcohol, coupled with the digestive benefits of some of the botanicals, encouraged consumption after dinner. Goldwasser was an early example that combined the benefits of gold, perceived to be an excellent cure-all, with caraway, to provide the best of digestives. Similarly peppermint, already known as an aid to digestion, was transformed into crème de menthe and became a popular digestive liqueur. More recently, the colours, exotic aromas and flavours of liqueurs have made significant contributions to the sensual enjoyment of mixed drinks and cocktails.

The word liqueur is derived from the Latin *lique-facere*, meaning to melt, make liquid, or dissolve.

DEFINITIONS OF LIQUEURS

Though grouped with other spirits, it is worth noting that liqueurs and spirits do differ in one important aspect. In the production of other spirits, natural sugars in the raw materials are transformed into alcohol and congeners whereas liqueurs are very often neutral or defined spirits to which sweeteners and flavourings are added. Generally, much of the character of a liqueur comes from these additions rather than from the raw materials. In other words, the spirit is used to enhance the other ingredients; examples of this are the whisky in Drambuie and the cognac in Grand Marnier. Other liqueurs, like Cointreau, result from the distillation of the raw material, just like other spirits.

The EU definition of a liqueur is fairly broad, encompassing any ethyl alcohol/distillate of agricultural origin, one or more spirit drinks or a mixture of both that has been sweetened and flavoured, to which products of agricultural origin may be added such as cream, milk or other milk products, fruit, wine or flavoured wine as defined by local regulation.

Flavourings and aromas can be natural or naturally synthesized but the latter is forbidden in the case of blackcurrant, raspberry, cherry, blueberry, citrus fruit, pineapple and plant liqueurs such as mint; in these cases, only natural flavourings may be used. Any colourings used must be permitted within the country of sale.

A liqueur's minimum alcoholic strength by volume is 15% ABV. Above this, the minimum levels of alcohol vary according to regulations specified for each category of liqueurs.

Generally, the minimum sugar content is 100 grams per litre, though with certain categories of liqueur other minimums apply. For cherry liqueurs, when the ethyl alcohol consists exclusively of cherry spirit, the minimum sugar content is 70 grams; for liqueurs prepared with gentian or similar plants as the sole aromatic substance, it is 80 grams; for egg liqueurs it is 150 grams; and for crème liqueurs it is 250 grams except for crème de cassis, when 400 grams is the minimum content.

Crèmes and creams are not the same. "Crème de..." indicates a liqueur with one dominant flavour, while a cream liqueur combines dairy cream with alcohol.

For historical reasons, compound terms including the word 'brandy' may be used to describe certain liqueurs such as prune, orange, apricot and cherry brandies even though they are produced in the European Community by blending ethyl alcohol of agricultural origin, rather than being brandy distilled from the designated fruit and sugar. Otherwise, to be called brandy, fruit spirits must be distilled from the fermented juice of the specified fruit. Only brandies distilled from grapes need not specify the fruit.

CLASSIFICATIONS OF LIQUEURS

The source of the base alcohol

- Neutral spirit from cereals, fruit or molasses
- Whisk(e)y
- Brandy from grapes
- Rum from sugar cane juice or molasses
- Fruit spirit
- Rice spirit

Historical French classifications

Historically, the French have classified liqueurs according to their sugar content and levels of alcohol:

- **Demi-fines** contain 200 to 250 grams of sugar and are bottled at a minimum of 23% ABV.

- **Fines** contain 400 to 450 grams of sugar and are bottled at a minimum of 28% ABV.

- **Surfines** contain 450 to 500 grams of sugar and are bottled at a minimum of 30% ABV.

- **Double** are identical to surfines in their levels of sugar and alcohol but they use greater quantities of flavourings.

Extraction methods

The methods used to extract essential oils from their raw materials can provide another means of classifying liqueurs.

Maceration means soaking the flavouring and colouring ingredients, usually in cold spirit. This could take a very long time but may be the only possible method of retaining the character and colour of some plants.

Infusion means soaking the flavouring, usually dried ingredients, in warm spirit. The nature and level of extraction depends upon the concentration and temperature of the solvent solution, though infusion is likely to be quicker and to extract more than maceration. After maceration and infusion, the extraction may be concentrated, compounded, distilled and/or matured.

Percolation means trickling the pure spirit, hot or cold, through the flavouring materials in columns or containers. This is a more efficient means of extraction than maceration. The process requires large quantities of spirit or use of a closed container in which a constant amount of spirit can be heated to boiling point and the vapours passed through the base material extracting the soluble compounds.

Distillation may be used alone or in addition to any of the above processes. Distillation is key to the extraction and concentration of defined fractions of a distillate and may be carried out under vacuum conditions if lower temperatures are required to protect delicate raw materials. Distillates are colourless, high in alcoholic strength, dry and will tend to be used when a certain finesse is required in a liqueur. As the distillates are dry, to be sold as liqueurs they require the addition of sugar. They may also need the addition of colour and subsequent dilution to reach the chosen bottling strength.

Maturation in wood mellows the spirit through oxidation and introduces additional flavours drawn from the wood or it may simply allow the distillate to develop extra complexity as the constituent parts marry.

Pressure means pressing raw materials such as fruit peel to extract the flavour.

Cold compounding means adding flavour essences or concentrates to a neutral or defined spirit. This process is used to produce liqueurs at lower cost. Flavourings are simply left to soak in a suitable alcohol to transfer the intended character. The level of alcohol is likely to be key to attaining specific standard flavours.

The skill of the compounder is vital in combining liquids obtained by any of the above methods; the sequence of mixing, the respective temperatures, the interaction of the materials and the alcohols all create reactions that should enhance the final product, but which could put at risk the desired results and any continuity of flavour.

Finally, sugar syrup is added together with a stabilizing agent if required, such as with cream liqueurs. The product is then rested to allow the constituent parts to marry, mostly in glass or in stainless steel but some in wood.

FLAVOURINGS

Flavourings are common to all liqueurs and their nature can provide another means of classification.

Mixed and single herbs, flowers and spices

These are some of the oldest and best known traditional liqueurs with some recipes dating back to the days when herbs and plants were added to a spirit as much for their perceived medicinal benefits as to mask the taste of the raw spirit. In abbeys and monasteries across Europe, distillation and the properties of herbs, plants and berries were researched with the aim of creating 'elixirs of life'. In so doing, they created numerous herb liqueurs, many of which remain with us today. These include Chartreuse, which has been produced by Carthusian monks since the seventeenth century, originally in their monastery near Grenoble, France, and now in a distillery using the herbal mixture prepared by two monks (two monks are always the sole custodians of the secret recipe); and Bénédictine, which dates back to 1510 and to the abbey near Fécamp, where the liqueur was claimed to revive tired monks when consumed in moderation and to fight the malarial diseases that were prevalent around the monastery.

Some recipes such as Drambuie have been passed down through generations and today remain the secrets of the families who developed them, while others like Strega are the subject of romantic legend. Some result from well over 100 different ingredients, while others reflect a single dominant herb flavour. Most offer significant digestive qualities.

Fruits

Fruit liqueurs, unlike those based on herbs, reflect the move to drinking for enjoyment rather than for medicinal benefits. Many fruit brandy liqueurs result from the fruits being macerated in brandy or even neutral spirit rather than from distillation. For example, terms such as cherry, apricot and peach brandy, are allowed for historical reasons, even though their base alcohol is neutral spirit. These are exceptions to the usual definition of brandies.

Fruit liqueurs can be made in the following ways:

- Fruit juice, pulp and flavourings can be compounded with a specified or neutral spirit and sugars added.

- Fruit can be macerated, infused or percolated with alcohol, with or without additional compounding. With stone fruits, the kernel may be included in these primary processes. The product may be sweetened and/or coloured.

- The fermented mash of the fruit (with or without kernels) may be distilled to produce an eau-de-vie fruit brandy.

- Some may add a small amount of fruit distillate to a fruit liqueur to lift the aromas and add extra finesse and elegance.

General classification of fruit liqueurs

- Berry

- Stone fruit

- Citrus fruit is the largest category: The term curaçao was initially used to describe liqueurs made from oranges from the island of Curaçao. But the term has since become generic to describe any liqueur in which the predominant flavour is derived from citrus fruit. The flesh of the fruit is discarded and only the peel is used. The dried peels are soaked in water and steeped in spirit before distillation extracts their flavours. The basic, dry, high strength curaçao can be compounded with water and sugar. Curaçaos are naturally clear. If colourings are added they are purely decorative. Triple sec has no definitive meaning but distillation using a double rectification would incur a three-stage production process.

- Tropical and other fruit

- Bean, seed, kernel and nut liqueurs. This category includes a wide range of liqueurs. The caraway seed, Europe's oldest cultivated spice, was the base of the first liqueur to be commercialized, when it was distilled and sweetened for sale as Kümmel by the Bols family in 1575. Chocolate liqueurs are produced by the maceration or percolation of cacao beans followed by distillation and sweetening. Coffee liqueurs are usually produced by the infusion in neutral or character spirit of coffee extract from their countries of origin, like Tia Maria and Jamaica; Kahlúa and Mexico; Toussaint and Haiti. Some are relatively dry like Toussaint with 250 grams of sugar, others are very sweet, like Kahlúa with nearer 500 grams. Almond/apricot-flavoured liqueurs like Amaretto may result from an infusion of bitter almond and apricot kernel oils rather than the nuts themselves, married with other herbs and fruits previously macerated in neutral alcohol. Frangelico is a hazelnut liqueur that also includes vanilla and cocoa. The coconut liqueurs like Malibu and Koko Kanu infuse coconut milk with neutral spirit or with rums.

- Dairy (milk, cream and eggs) liqueurs include advocaat, a thick, custard-like, creamy liqueur derived from a drink made in the Dutch colonies in South America, using avocado. Today advocaat is made from the yolks of eggs mixed with brandy, sugar and vanilla. Cream liqueurs, the most successful category of liqueurs since the launch of Baileys in the 1970s, combine a base spirit and maybe a specified spirit with cream, sugar and flavourings.

- Mistelle is a French word used to describe a fresh fruit juice or a part-fermented fruit juice to which a matching spirit is added to bring the fermentation to a halt. Because all the fruit sugars remain or only small amounts have been converted into alcohol, mistelles are very sweet and usually served as a base for apéritifs. These include: Pineau des Charentes, a mixture of grape juice and cognac; Floc de Gascogne, grape juice and armagnac; and Pommeau de Normandie made from apple juice and calvados.

- Ratafias are French-based mistelles, historically consumed at the ratification of treaties. Similar products exist in Spain, Portugal and Italy.

- Crèmes de ... is a French term that does not imply that the liqueur contains cream but that one specified flavour predominates. Double crème, as in double crème de cassis, suggests double the flavour component. However 50% extra is more usual as the essential oils in many ingredients can cause cloudiness when too concentrated and diluted with water or sugar and water. So 'double' doesn't necessarily mean double. The term 'double crème de cassis de Dijon' is banned.

Quiz on liqueurs

1. Which of these towns became renowned as a centre for cassis production?

    A. Annecy
    B. Marseille
    C. Nancy
    D. Dijon

2. Imports of fruit into which of these ports prompted the production of curaçao?

    A. Amsterdam
    B. Trieste
    C. Marseille
    D. Barcelona

3. Which family claims to have first commercialized liqueur production?

    A. Marie Brizard
    B. De Kuyper
    C. Bols
    D. Briottet

4. What is the minimum sugar content per litre for classification as a liqueur?

    A. 50 grams

B. 100 grams
C. 150 grams
D. 200 grams

5. What is the minimum sugar content per litre for classification
    as a crème, except crème de cassis?

    A. 150
    B. 200
    C. 250
    D. 300

6. Which of these production methods would result in a dry,
    colourless spirit?

    A. Maceration
    B. Infusion
    C. Percolation
    D. Distillation

7. Curaçao is a term used to describe a liqueur predominantly
    flavoured with what?

    A. Citrus fruits
    B. Spices
    C. Herbs
    D. Beans

8. Which would be the correct description of a fruit juice mixed
    with a matching spirit such as apple juice and calvados?

    A. Eau-de-vie
    B. Liqueur
    C. Mistelle
    D. Fruit brandy

1. D; 2. A; 3. C; 4. B; 5. C; 6. D; 7. A; 8. C

Answers

11

EAUX-DE-VIE

BACKGROUND

Eaux-de-vie is the term used for brandies destined to become cognac or armagnac, but it is also the name of the dry, true fruit distillates made from fruits other than grapes, usually bottled at higher strength than liqueurs, between 40% and 45% ABV, and sometimes aged. These are generally classified according to whether made from soft or stone fruit. All eaux-de-vie are unsweetened, clean and fresh in character which means that the fruit used must always be ripe and untainted, which is costly as it takes around 100 kilos of fruit to make five to ten litres of fruit spirit.

The Alpine triangle in Europe is a major area for production of eaux-de-vie. This includes the Black Forest in southern Germany, the Alsace region, the Swiss valleys, Austria and north-east Italy across to the Balkans.

Fermentation is usually as long as nature requires to capture as much flavour as possible. Distillation can be executed in pots to relatively low levels of alcohol to preserve the character of the fruit or in continuous stills to higher levels of alcohol in order to highlight the more fragrant aromatics and to eliminate methanol, levels of which can be significant in some fruits.

Most are bottled immediately to preserve character, resting only if settling is necessary, in glass or stainless steel. They are usually colourless. Generally, only those distilled from stone fruits are aged, for example, slivovitz from the Balkans is made from plums and ground kernels that are crushed and pressed before fermentation and then distilled and matured in wood to refine the overall quality.

The division between soft and stone fruit reflects the fact that soft fruits, including pear, are low in sugar. They must first be chopped and macerated in neutral spirit to produce sufficient alcohol for distillation. One example is a raspberry flavoured spirit called himbeergeist, which cannot be produced by fermenting raspberries because their low sugar content yields too little alcohol. Instead, neutral alcohol is infused with the raspberries. The mixture is diluted and redistilled. Some may choose not to macerate in this way but to ferment the soft fruit; the results can be excellent but the yield will be very low.

Stone fruits, like cherries, will not need prior maceration as they contain enough sugar to ferment into fruit wine ready for distillation. Some distillers may choose to crack and crush kernels with the fruits to add a pleasant bitterness to the distillate.

APPLE BRANDY

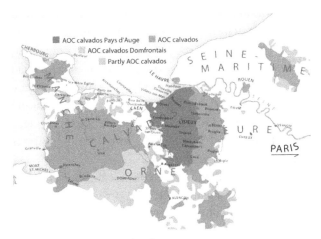

Map of the appellations of calvados

The French apple brandy called calvados, is named after the Normandy region of Calvados and dates back to the sixteenth century. Today, it is distilled by a large number of small artisan distillers in eleven defined areas of Normandy, all of which enjoy AOC (appellation d'origine contrôlée) status. Of these areas, two, Pays d'Auge and Domfrontais, warrant more restrictive AOC status.

A blend of different apples is usually used to make the various house styles.

- Sweet apples provide the sugars for fermentation to convert into alcohol.

- Bitter apples provide the tannins for taste and aroma.

- Bitter-sweet apples provide sugar and tannins.

- Tart, sour and acidic apples provide freshness and help to stabilize the cider.

Fermentation is natural, using yeasts from the skin of the fruit and lasts from one to three months, resulting in a cider of around 4%–6% ABV. Distillation takes place from the start of winter through to June 30th in the following year. The low initial level of alcohol results in a heavy concentration of flavours as the alcohol level rises towards 70% ABV. Distillation can be in pot or column stills, except in Pays d'Auge where only pot stills may be used. In Domfrontais only column stills may be used and at least 30% of the brandy must be distilled from pears grown around the town of Domfront in lower Normandy.

Calvados must be aged in oak barrels for a minimum of two years, except calvados Domfrontais, which must be aged for a minimum of three years. There are no rules on the nature of wood nor on the size of barrel.

Usually, batches are blended for consistency, but vintages can be found. Most blend with water to reach bottling strength. But some producers allow the alcohol to evaporate to bottling strength. The age on the bottle refers to the youngest component.

CLASSIFICATIONS

- **XXX** must be aged for a minimum of two years for calvados and three years for calvados Domfrontais.

- **Vieux, Reserve** and similar descriptions mean that the product has been aged for at least three years.

- **VO, Vieille Reserve** and **VSOP** require at least four years ageing.

- **XO, Hors d'Age** and **Napoleon** must be aged at least six years but most are usually older.

- **Produit Fermier** means all the fruit is estate grown at the distillery.

According to legend, during their meals, Normans drank a glass of calvados between courses to aid digestion and to sharpen appetites for the remainder of the repast. This custom of making space for more food is called the *trou Norman*, or the Norman hole, and continues to this day.

OTHER APPLE BRANDIES

Cider brandy was taxed out of existence in the seventeenth century in England but production resumed in the 1980s. Now there are several English cider brandies.

In America, cider brandy is distilled mainly in New England, where the early settlers discovered that hops did not grow well but apple trees did. The brandy distilled there is called applejack and the best is distilled in pots and matured in oak for at least two years. It is generally light in flavour and aroma, particularly those that are blends of around 35% cider brandy and 65% neutral spirit.

Quiz on eaux-de-vie

1. The so-called 'Alpine triangle' is noted for production of what style of spirit?

   A. Eaux-de-vie
   B. Cassis
   C. Absinthe
   D. Herb liqueurs

2. Which of these fruits would usually be macerated in neutral spirit prior to distillation into an eau-de-vie?

   A. Plum
   B. Cherry
   C. Raspberry
   D. Apple

3. Distillation must be executed in pots in which Calvados region?

   A. Domfrontais
   B. Pays d'Auge
   C. All Calvados regions
   D. Caen

4. In the Domfrontais region of Calvados 30% of the brandy must be distilled from what fruit?

   A. Pear
   B. Grape
   C. Sweet apple
   D. Bitter apple

5. Calvados must be aged for a minimum of how many years?

   A. One year
   B. Two years
   C. Three years
   D. Four years

6. Applejack is distilled in which country?

A. Germany

B. England

C. Canada

D. America

12

IRISH WHISKEY

BACKGROUND TO IRISH WHISKEY

Ireland is agreed by most to have been the birthplace of whiskey and, to this day, Irish whiskey remains equal to all. These are whiskeys of outstanding finesse and quality.

Consumption of the 'water of life' has been documented many times, but the origins of Irish whiskey are unknown. No document has ever been found to authenticate either the place or the time of its first appearance. An early record of a drink that could be whiskey can be found in the *Annals of Ireland by the Four Masters for Connaught,* in which it is recorded that Risteard Mac Raghnaill fell into a coma one Christmas evening in 1405 after drinking *esci bethad* to excess and it was a deadly water to him. *The Red Book of Ossory,* dating from the early sixteenth century, records *uisce beathe* being produced for consumption and by the end of that century, Irish whiskey had certainly become a favourite of Elizabeth I of England. Sir Walter Raleigh also took a couple of casks on his travels. In Tudor times the English were expressing concerns about the damage aqua vitae, distilled from grain, was doing to the Irish people and so it was clear, by this time at least, that the Irish were drinking whiskey.

Following the Tudor settlement of Ireland the Crown began to extract revenues from the Irish people and in 1608, on behalf of the Crown, the Lord Deputy of Ireland granted the first Irish whiskey patent, not to control production or consumption but to raise revenue. Soon the monopolies these patents granted became riddled with corruption and the system was close to collapse so in 1661 these patents were abolished in exchange for a tax on every gallon of whiskey distilled. The tax was introduced on Christmas Day and by Boxing Day illegal production of whiskey had begun. For another century, corruption, deception and tax evasion made any proper record of whiskey production in Ireland impossible. What is certain, however, is that the international reputation of 'Irish' continued to grow. It was the choice of the Russian Tsar Peter the Great, who declared of all the wines, 'the Irish spirit is the best' and, in 1755, in the first English dictionary, Dr Johnson described *usquebaugh* as an Irish word, which signifies the waters of life. It is a 'compounded, distilled spirit being drawn of aromatiks, and the Irish sort is particularly distinguished for its pleasant and mild flavour. The highland sort is somewhat hotter and by corruption in Scotch is called whisky.'

This confirms that, by this time, *usquebaugh* or 'water of life' refers explicitly to whiskey and that, in Ireland, it was mixed with aromatics just as scotch was flavoured with herbs. This definition also confirms that the Scottish word, whisky, was a corruption of the Irish word, suggesting Irish whisky pre-dated scotch.

The popularity of Irish whiskey grew in Britain and its colonies so that by 1779 the Irish House of Commons recorded 1,152 distilleries. Many more were not registered, meaning tax collection on the volumes of whiskey distilled was far from successful. In 1779, the English government again changed the system to one that taxed the stills instead of production in order to guarantee them a set income, but within a year the number of registered stills had dropped by 80%. The few that did pay their taxes were obliged to drive their stills so hard and fast to remain competitive that the quality of their whiskey plummeted.

Their so-called 'Parliament whiskey' gained the reputation of rot-gut compared with the whiskeys produced by illegal distillers that were referred to as *poteen*. By 1823 the number of registered distilleries operating in Ireland dropped to only forty and an Act of Parliament overhauled the tax system yet again to tax only production. The effects were immediate.

By 1840, the number of registered stills had risen to eighty-six and, by 1867, what remains the world's largest pot still was operating at Midleton distillery. Irish whiskeys were now being sold in very large quantities to satisfy global demand. What's more, the whiskey they produced was, by now, sufficiently consistent in quality for distillers in Dublin, like John Power and John Jameson, to put their names on their bottles as guarantees of quality. Irish distilleries consolidated and expanded and by 1850, Irish was outselling scotch in Scotland and, prior to Prohibition, Irish was the whiskey of choice in America, outselling scotch there, too.

When Alfred Barnard toured Ireland in 1885, he recorded that the big four distilleries in Dublin were huge and boasted a combined output in excess of five million gallons a year. This compared with an average of less than 100,000 gallons per distillery in Scotland.

A WHISKEY IN DECLINE

The decline of Irish whiskey is well documented. At the beginning of the eighteenth century, the British government introduced the Corn Laws to protect British landowners. These laws banned the importation of grain into Ireland and Britain. Gradually, they drove many of the Irish to poverty and, thanks to the potato famine in 1845, ultimately to America.

In another blow to whiskey drinking, in 1840 a Capuchin Friar named Father Matthew was campaigning successfully against alcohol, the demon drink; encouraged by his crusade, 60% of the population vowed total abstinence. Over one third of public houses closed and many smaller distilleries had to shut down, leaving larger distilleries to grow at their expense.

In 1827, Robert Stein, a Scots distiller, had invented the process of continuous distillation. By 1831, Aeneas Coffey, a French-born, retired Irish excise officer had improved and patented this process, introducing the two parallel columns, the analyzer and the rectifier. Initially the Irish rejected this invention, but the Scots did not. Most probably the Scots did not recognize the column still as a provider of potable spirit for whisky production either. More likely they saw it as an investment to be made in their lowland distilleries to enable them to provide cheap spirit for the booming gin producers south of the border.

By the end of the nineteenth century a number of Irish distillers, particularly in the north, had embraced this new invention and grown rapidly alongside the scotch blenders. Tyrconnell was one such whiskey to enjoy immense success in America well into the twentieth century. However, threatened by the large-scale Irish distillers, the scotch distillers joined together in a trust and, to protect their position, simply bought up many Irish distilleries, leaving only the traditional and small pot distilleries to continue to operate.

These traditional Irish distillers, mainly based in Dublin, still refused to adopt the Coffey still, continuing to believe that their success depended on the full-flavoured whiskeys distilled in the pot, even though they had to be sold at a significant premium compared to the new blends. They had no wish to dilute or adulterate their whiskeys. Though they failed to stem the decline of Irish whiskey overall, in that decision lay the reasons for the survival and strong position of pot-still whiskeys in the overall sales of Irish whiskey during the twentieth and twenty-first centuries.

Robert Peel repealed the Corn Laws in 1846. American corn, once again, became available to distillers. Unfortunately for the Irish, availability of cheap corn now permitted the Scots to use the Coffey still for large-scale production of high percentage alcohol even more profitably.

A new law permitting whiskey to be stored in bonded warehouses with the tax to be paid only on shipment failed to impress the Irish with its potential benefits. In Scotland, however, the merchants recognized that this law permitted them to buy the malts and the higher alcohol grain whiskies from the Coffey stills, blend the two together and bottle and label them as their own brands before having to pay any tax.

In 1853 Andrew Usher, created the first, so-called vatted whisky and others, like William Teacher and the Chivas brothers, quickly followed his example. Their scotch blends sold around the world at the expense of Irish whiskey, while the Irish distillers continued to claim these so-called silent spirits from the Scottish blenders could not justify the description of whisky and so ought not to be sold under that name.

In the 1870s the phylloxera blight destroyed vines in France and supplies of French brandy dried up. By now, the Coffey still was producing a considerable quantity of grain spirit in Ireland. But it was the scotch blenders, the so-called 'whisky barons' rather than the Irish distillers, who took advantage of the new gap in the market and positioned their new scotch blends to satisfy the demand for a drink to replace cognac in the colonies. The Scots also took every opportunity to introduce their blends into Ireland.

The traditional Dublin distillers remained convinced that their pot-still whiskeys would see the Coffey still off. Instead, many in England and Scotland took advantage of the reputation of Irish whiskeys and shipped inferior malts and grain whiskies as counterfeit Irish whiskey. It did not help the Irish that they tended to sell in cask to middlemen, denying them all opportunities to brand their whiskeys until well into the twentieth century.

Despite this, during the nineteenth century, Irish whiskey continued to outsell scotch. But then circumstances combined to ensure that sales of Irish whiskey would plummet. From the 1860s to the 1930s, as politics took their toll, Irish whiskey's share of world whisk(e)y sales fell from 60% to 10% and less. Eventually, during the twentieth century it dropped to as low as 2%. The Easter Rising in Dublin, in 1916, followed by the Irish War of Independence, from 1919 to 1921, ending in partition and the Civil War (1922–1923) resulted in many disputes with Britain over the repatriation of land rents. These disputes lasted from 1923 to 1933 and during this time all opportunity for the sale of Irish whiskey was denied in Britain as well as throughout the British Empire. What is more, Irish distillers received little if any encouragement from the new Irish Free State.

From 1919 until 1933, Prohibition in America denied the Irish a market where their share had been as high as 75%. Worse, its reputation as a premium whiskey ensured plenty of 'Irish' was bootlegged only to damage that reputation over time.

Real Irish whiskey was not shipped until after Prohibition even though Joseph Kennedy, father of US President John, had requested shipments, only to be informed that the Irish had no wish to break the law. In contrast, the Scots and Canadians maintained supplies throughout Prohibition. So, when the 'great experiment' came to an end, tastes had swung to these countries' lighter styles of whisky.

During the Second World War and until 1953, the Irish government restricted whiskey exports in order to maintain domestic revenues whereas Winston Churchill encouraged production of scotch to fuel foreign sales and to boost foreign earnings.

These circumstances combined to ensure that Irish whiskey went into free-fall while the Scottish blenders achieved global status for their brands of scotch. As demand for whisk(e)y grew in the twentieth century, scotch, not Irish, was positioned to become the whisk(e)y of choice around the world.

THE RESTORATION OF IRISH WHISKEY

During the twentieth century, distillery numbers continued to decline. In 1966, three of the remaining four distilleries, Jameson, Powers and Cork distilleries combined to form Irish Distillers, and Bushmills followed in 1973. In 1968, Jameson switched from being a pure pot-still whiskey to a blend and Irish whiskey began to compete with scotch as branded, blended whiskeys. In 1988, the Pernod-Ricard Group bought Irish Distillers and committed to restoring Irish whiskey's fortunes, specifically through the global development of Jameson. Pernod-Ricard remained Ireland's only whiskey producer until 1989 when John Teeling reopened the Cooley Distillery and began independent distillation of Irish whiskey.

More recently, with the purchase of Tullamore Dew by Cantrell and Cochrane in 1994, the purchase of Cantrell and Cochrane by William Grant, the acquisition of Bushmills first by Diageo and then by Jose Cuervo, the expanding portfolio of Cooley, bought by Jim Beam in 2011, the continuing strength of Irish Distillers as well as the decision of William Grant and others to build new distilleries in Ireland, investment has flowed into Ireland and Irish whiskey is regaining recognition for its individuality, variety and quality.

IRISH COFFEE

Throughout the second half of the twentieth century it was an Irish coffee drink, rather than the whiskey itself, that maintained any recognition for Irish whiskey.

From the 1930s flying boats en route from Russia to America landed to refuel at Foynes airport on the River Shannon in county Limerick. In 1942, one flight turned back and the tired, cold passengers were greeted by the barman Joe Sheridan. He offered them a glass of hot black coffee mixed with brown demerara sugar and Irish whiskey, topped with ice cold cream.

In 1952 Stanton Delaplane, a San Francisco newspaper columnist, stopped off at the world's first duty-free shop, across the estuary at Shannon, the airport that had replaced Foynes. Seduced by the same drink, he took the recipe home to Fisherman's Wharf and introduced it to the local Buena Vista Café.

Irish Coffee became the worldwide hit that it has remained ever since. Regrettably, however, its success only served to encourage a perception of Irish as the whiskey to mix with coffee, while the reputation of scotch as the whisky of choice continued to go from strength to strength.

WHISKEY WITH AN 'E'

In the nineteenth century, possibly to distinguish their whiskey from the column distilled Scotch whiskies, those distilled in Dublin were spelt with an 'e'. This practice also distinguished Dublin pot-still whiskeys from their rural competitors and from Irish Coffey-still whiskies. Since the formation of Irish Distillers in 1966 all Irish whiskey has been spelt this way.

WHERE IS IRISH WHISKEY PRODUCED?

Irish is a whiskey distilled in a climate matched in no other country. Bushmills is situated in the north where the weather is damp and wet and the water is hard. Cooley is distilled in the damp east, using the soft local spring water. In the south, at Midleton, the giant stills stand in hot and humid warehouses with the warm Gulf Stream flowing nearby, causing occasional palm trees to sway in the breeze. Here the water is soft.

In 2007, when the distillery celebrated its 250th anniversary, whiskey production began again at Kilbeggan, in the Midlands' province of Leinster.

The Midleton distillery

This is a complex facility with a high production capacity, situated close to Cork. The distillery uses a variety of pot and column stills, able to be linked in any combination, to triple distil a variety of different distillates. Each will then be aged separately before vatting to deliver any number of specific brand styles. Outside the distillery, though no longer in use, stands the world's largest pot still with a staggering volume of 141,000 litres.

Midleton distils a full range of whiskeys, from grain to pure pot-still whiskeys. The malt is not dried with peat smoke but in closed kilns fired by gas. All can be matured in different woods, before being vatted in varying proportions to produce the consistent whiskeys required and defined by their brands. To this purpose, Midleton pioneered the production of casks to meet its specific needs, whether in ex-bourbon American oak or European oak previously used to age sherry, port or madeira.

The Bushmills distillery

Records suggest that whiskey may have been produced in this region as early as 1276, but the Bushmills distillery was founded in 1784, not in 1608 when James I of England granted a licence to distil in this area to Sir Thomas Philips. The distinctive pagoda roofs were introduced in the late 1800s to improve the draught through the kiln.

By the end of the 1700s, Bushmills was producing close to 50,000 litres of whiskey, most of which went to America and the West Indies.

Today Bushmills produces only malt whiskeys, using barley grown in Ireland. One malt style is not smoked to allow the natural taste of the barley to carry through while another is lightly peated. The delicate Bushmills whiskeys are distilled in pot stills that promote lots of copper conversation and plenty of reflux. The grain whiskey used in Bushmills' blends comes from the Midleton distillery.

The Cooley distillery

The distillery was set up in the 1930s to produce methylated spirit from diseased potatoes. In the 1980s it diversified and produced potable spirit for the likes of Baileys and Smirnoff. In 1987 a company founded by John Teeling bought it and set up Ireland's first independent distillery in more than 100 years. The Cooley distillery was able to fill its first cask two years later. Soon after, Cooley distillery bought the right to use two dormant whiskey brands, Kilbeggan and Locke's. Apart from these two brands, Cooley also owns Tyrconnell single malt, Connemara peated single malt and Millar's Irish whiskey.

For malt whiskey, Cooley use two relatively small copper pot stills with uncharacteristically long necks. The new-make spirit is double distilled to below 70% ABV, similar to the practice in Scotland to produce a whiskey closer to the Scottish than to the traditional Irish style.

The grain whiskey, distilled in patent stills, uses corn to provide a rich sweet centre to the Cooley blends.

After distillation the raw spirit is transported to the old Locke's distillery in Kilbeggan, where Cooley restarted production in 2007. Here, the spirit is aged in mostly first-fill, ex-bourbon barrels. All Cooley whiskeys are chill-filtered except for Connemara cask strength.

IRISH WHISKEY PRODUCTION

In Ireland, it is neither the climate nor the master blender that defines the whiskey. Rather the distiller exerts the most influence on the finished product, using varying distillation processes to create the building blocks of four styles of whiskey: pure pot still, blends, single malts and single grain. Pure pot-still whiskey is unique to Ireland.

In blends, introduced only in the second half of the twentieth century, the main grain is corn, the ingredient that gives Irish its typical, tongue-coating character of buttered popcorn.

Pure pot-still whiskey, however, is not only distilled in pot stills but the mash is made up only of malted and unmalted barley and this is key to the traditional individuality of Irish whiskey. Historically, the mash would have included other cereals like oats but in the nineteenth century, to save paying the taxes imposed by the English on malted barley, the Irish decided to use some unmalted barley in their mash. The unmalted barley saved the distillers money but it also changed the character of the whiskey, helping to generate a spicy, fruity taste and an oily firmness on the palate that served to balance the softness of the malted barley.

Today, only a few Irish whiskeys, such as Green Spot and Redbreast, are bottled as traditional pure pot-still whiskeys. Most Irish whiskeys are now blends but the contribution made by the pot-still whiskey is key to the overall quality of these blends. In a standard blend, the minimum content is 30% and the usual proportion will be 40% to 60%.

During the eighteenth and nineteenth centuries, distillers in the country areas probably used peat, but production became concentrated in larger distilleries situated in towns where peat was not the usual fuel. For this reason, grains are generally dried in sealed kilns and not smoked over peat, unlike the situation in Scotland, so the grain flavours are likely to be more noticeable. The yeasts are standard but germination lasts as long as sixty to 100 hours, creating numerous flavour compounds for distillation to concentrate.

In the nineteenth century some Irish distillers had adopted triple distillation to compete with the lighter scotch blends, and by the time Irish whiskeys emerged from their early twentieth-century crises most were triple distilled. A wash still is used to remove heavier compounds and then an intermediate and finally a spirit still are used to refine the distillate. The pot fills and the spirit cuts vary to deliver the many different whiskey building blocks required by the distiller.

Single malt whiskey is made only from malted barley and it is rarely peated; the majority is produced by the Bushmills and Cooley distilleries.

Grain whiskey is column distilled from corn and a small percentage of malted barley. Most is used in Irish blends, though at least one single grain whiskey is bottled.

Cooley uses a double column Coffey still, whereas Midleton uses continuous distillation and all its stills are linked together to allow for triple and even multiple distillation. This facility also allows for the diversion of distillates of malted and unmalted barley into the continuous process to provide the distiller with extra 'building block' options.

Irish whiskey uses a variety of woods for maturation and usually wood from barrels that have already held other spirits or wines. The usual choice is ex-bourbon casks made from American oak but sherry, rum or port casks can be used for a finish in the later years of ageing. New wood is not usual because it would likely overwhelm other elements in the whiskey's flavour profile but interaction between the spirit and the seasoned wood can generate as much as 50% of the final whiskey's flavour.

Irish whiskey must be aged in wood for at least three years and, before bottling, a process called vatting allows the whiskeys to marry in giant holding tanks for just a few days or for as long as a month. Because of Ireland's proximity to the Gulf Stream that carries warm, damp air from Florida, the climate in southern Ireland is warm and the whiskeys mature there more quickly than in the north or in Scotland.

Around 0.5% caramel may be added to offset the variables that can affect the whiskey's final colour.

The whiskey is normally chill-filtered before bottling.

Quiz on Irish whiskeys

1. Which ruler claimed Irish whiskey to be the best?

   A. James I of England
   B. Peter the Great of Russia
   C. Louis XVI of France
   D. Philip V of Spain

2. In which year did an Act of Parliament overhaul the tax system and establish foundations for the Irish whiskey market that exists today?

   A. 1789
   B. 1801
   C. 1823
   D. 1850

3. In 1885 the four Dublin distillers boasted an annual production of 5 million gallons plus. At the time, this compared with an average of how many gallons per distillery in Scotland?

   A. One hundred thousand
   B. One million
   C. Five million
   D. Ten million

4. Who was the Irish excise officer who perfected and patented the process of continuous distillation?

   A. Robert Stein
   B. John Power
   C. Robert Peel
   D. Aeneas Coffey

5. What was the name of the barman at Foynes airport who created and served the first Irish Coffee?

   A. Stanton Delaplane
   B. Joe Kennedy

C. Joe Sheridan
D. Paddy Murphy

6. Which of these Irish whiskeys combines malted and unmalted barley in the mash?

A. Malt whiskey
B. Pot-still whiskey
C. Grain whiskey
D. All of these

13

AMERICAN WHISK(E)Y

BACKGROUND TO AMERICAN WHISK(E)Y

In 1876, three years before any beer arrived, the cowboys of Dodge City were provided with no less than nineteen whiskey-selling outlets. By the next century the Temperance movement threatened the very existence of American whiskey.

The first formal pledge to abstain from spirits was taken in New York in 1808 and in 1826 the first pledge to totally abstain from alcohol was taken in Boston. In 1851, Maine became the first state to ban the sale of liquor and the movement was only temporarily marginalized during the American Civil War in the 1860s before moderation and temperance grew into a drive towards Prohibition after that war.

By 1910, 45% of America was dry and in 1917 whiskey production ceased in order to prioritize industrial alcohol for the war. Prohibition was in force three years later, in 1920. Although Prohibition was repealed in 1933, two-thirds of Kentucky remains dry as does the town of Lynchburg in Tennessee, home of Jack Daniel's. Worse for American whiskey, during Prohibition more spirits were drunk than ever before but the whisky was all imported from Canada or Scotland, so by 1933 Americans had become accustomed to the lighter style of these whiskies.

American distilleries were shut down again during World War Two and so by the 1950s American whiskey had suffered from more than fifty years of temperance and almost twenty years of no production at all. Were it not for these circumstances of history, there is every reason to believe that by the twenty-first century American whiskey could have been a significant global and domestic competitor to scotch.

The first printed recipe for bourbon appeared in 1813 and in 1821 the first advertisement for whiskey appeared in the *Western Citizen* newspaper, in Bourbon County, but it was not until 1964 that, even in America, bourbon gained due recognition, declared then by Act of Congress, to be 'America's native spirit'.

From the 1960s and well into the 1980s the preference was for bland drinks, epitomized by vodka, but towards the end of the twentieth century, tastes began to swing back towards flavour. Kentucky bourbon, Tennessee whiskey and, more recently, even American rye whiskey have become popular not only in America but around the world. The full-bodied style and varied character of these whiskeys encourage their enjoyment long or short, straight or on ice, refreshed with cola or mixed in classic cocktails and, most recently, even sipped, proving that Scotland is no longer the source of all good whiskies.

ORIGINS OF KENTUCKY BOURBON

Distilling came to America along with the Scots and Irish as they were driven from their homelands to America. Rye was a grain with which they were already familiar, making it the natural choice when these early settlers began to distil the first American whiskeys. Pennsylvania, Virginia and Maryland became the pioneer states for this rye whiskey because winning independence in 1789 required Washington to raise taxes to pay for the war effort and, to escape the taxes, the early distillers accelerated their trek west into these states.

In Kentucky the earliest records of distilling date from the eighteenth century, after Daniel Boone led fellow pioneers through the Cumberland Gap. In 1776, to encourage further settlement, the Governor of the State of Virginia offered 400 acres of free land to any man who agreed to move to the western part of Virginia, build a house and a farm and raise the native Indian corn (maize) and, after the War of Independence, these pioneers were joined by many of the Scottish and Irish distillers seeking to escape Washington's taxes.

These are the reasons why Bourbon and Tennessee, the two great American whiskeys of today, are both made further south, far from the original colonies and beyond the Appalachian mountains in a land covered with fields of the local Indian corn, a grain that grew faster and yielded more than any Old World grain. Though not known at the time, this land was also sitting on a limestone shelf that ensured the waters were naturally hard, iron-free and rich in the calcium that would prove to be ideal for making whiskey.

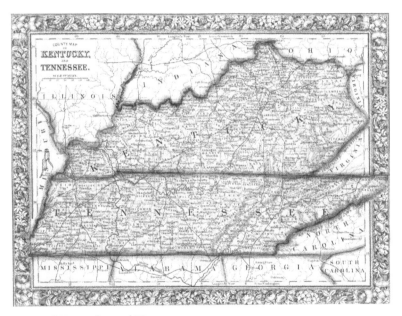

Map of Kentucky and Tennessee

By the 1780s, much of the annual corn crop was excess to family needs and some farmers turned into farmer distillers, routinely adding corn to their traditional rye formula. Soon, much of the spirit they produced also became excess to local need and, not being equipped to transport the barrels east over the Appalachian Mountains, early distillers chose to ship them down the Mississippi river to New

Orleans, which proved to be another decision that would help to define bourbon's future individuality.

It was not possible to ship the barrels downriver during the winter and so they rested in wood during these months before taking many more weeks to drift south down the river as summer temperatures rose. The distillers had charred their barrels, most probably because they knew burning the wood would help to remove the smells and other unwanted character remaining from their previous use. What they were less likely to know was that the heat of charring served to draw the colour and the vanillin from deep down in the local white oak to lie as a sweet, reddish sap, just below the char. Those weeks in wood and the extremes of temperature in the summer caused the 'white dog' (the name given to the new spirit that was colourless and raw enough to bite you) to move in and out of the pores in the wood, absorbing the sap through the char. On arrival in New Orleans, the white dog had become rich in colour and sweet in taste, the two characteristics now recognized to be distinctive hallmarks of the flavoursome, colourful and complex bourbon whiskeys that continue to benefit from Kentucky's extremes of temperature and the microclimates created in the warehouses.

Originally part of Virginia, in 1792 Kentucky became the fifteenth state of the Union and among the early pioneers in this region can be found some of the famous whiskey families whose names are still to be seen on bottles today: Elijah Pepper (Old Crow), Robert Samuels (ancestor to Bill Samuels Sr and creator of Makers' Mark), Basil Hayden (inspiration for Old Grand-Dad), Evan Williams, Jacob Böhm whose grandson, Jim Beam was born in 1864, and the Brown family (Old Forester). This family bought Jack Daniel's in 1956 for just $18 million. Until the middle of the nineteenth century many of these early whiskey makers remained farmer distillers rather than full-time distillers.

AMERICAN BLENDED AND STRAIGHT WHISKEYS

The invention of the continuous still in the 1830s had distillers in Scotland, Ireland and America questioning how blends could justify using the word 'whiskey', the same description used by malts. Scottish malt distillers and American distillers took the blenders to court but only in America did a law, the 1909 Bottled in Bond Act, oblige clear differentiation between straight and blended whiskeys.

American blended whiskeys are typically at least two straight bourbons and/or rye whiskeys blended together with a maximum of 80% neutral grain spirit or light whiskey, so called if the neutral spirit has been matured in used oak barrels or new ones without char. Unlike the grain spirit that must be matured for at least three years if used in blended scotch, regulations for American blended whiskey specify no minimum age for the grain spirit.

These whiskeys must be labeled 'blended' in letters as big as those used for the word 'whiskey'. They are usually quite smooth and delicate, lacking complexity and usually short in their finish. Their colour and flavour can be enhanced with the addition of up to 2.5% sherry. Only a blended whiskey containing at least 51% straight bourbon can be called blended bourbon whiskey.

Post-Prohibition, when stocks of matured American whiskey were low and tastes had been seduced by imports of the softer style of Canadian whisky, American blended whiskey was able to satisfy the growing demand for spirits suitable for combining with mixers in so-called 'highballs'.

American straight whiskeys are very different. They must be the product of one distillery, distilled to less than 80% ABV and, unlike with Scotch, Canadian and Irish, less flavoursome grain spirits drawn off the still at higher levels of alcohol are not permitted. In fact, most straights will exit the still at much lower levels of alcohol than 80% ABV, meaning that what is special about American straight whiskey versus other whiskeys is that the taste of the grains in the recipe is very noticeable.

Straights, excepting straight corn, must be aged for a minimum of two years in oak. The law does not specify use of American white oak, but it is the usual choice. The summers are very hot in both Kentucky and Tennessee and so maturation is more rapid in these states than in Scotland.

BOURBON VERSUS OTHER STRAIGHT WHISK(E)YS

Bourbon whiskey takes its name from Bourbon County in Kentucky because it was from this county's port at Limestone that the early barrels of whiskey were shipped down the Ohio River for sale in New Orleans. Bourbon County was named in 1785 in honour of Louis XVI of France's ruling family, the Bourbons, who had supported the colonists during their War of Independence. The recipients in New Orleans tasted the whiskey which had rested in wood for many months, and liked it. They sent back orders for more of the bourbon whiskey, using the name on the barrels that designated the port of loading. Its popularity could also have stemmed from the fact that New Orleans had a sizeable French population at the time. The name of this whiskey would certainly have appealed to them and the colour and character drawn from the wood would not have been too far removed from what they were familiar with in cognac.

The term bourbon denotes how the whiskey is made, not where it comes from, but bourbon cannot be produced in any other country except America where it can be made anywhere so long as the whiskey is made according to the rules regarding the mash bill, yeast, distillation process and maturation. These rules safeguard the whiskey's reputation for strong flavours and rich colour but they also provide ample opportunity for improvisation which is why bourbon is very much the individual product of each distiller.

The rules

The main grain, corn, must make up at least 51% of the mash although most distillers use between 70% and 80%. Corn is cheap and produces one third more starch than either wheat or rye, it combines well with the caramels and vanillin drawn from the wood and it also contributes sweet and oily flavours which help to define the rich, buttery nature of bourbon. Generally, however, the higher the percentage of corn used in the mash, the fatter the bourbon and, the less complex the overall taste.

Whether barley, rye or wheat, the percentages of small grains that each distiller chooses to enter into the mash, are chosen like seasoning selected by a cook. Malted barley converts the starch into sugar and, despite the relatively low quantities added into the mash, the barley can also contribute occasional biscuit notes. Rye provides a characteristic spicy bite and wheat generates a less traditional, delicate softness. Whichever the distiller's choice the contribution of small grains to the overall character and finish tends to develop over time, adding complexity to the initial taste of corn that can be dominant in the spirit that exits the still.

Grains are cooked to hydrolyze the starch, using water naturally filtered through the limestone shelf that is unique to the Kentucky and Tennessee states and which removes the irons so harmful to whiskey production while enriching the distillate with calcium.

Fermentation usually takes up to three days to reach around 5%–6% ABV and each distiller ferments using his own treasured strain of proprietary yeast. Four Roses bourbon has no less than five yeasts, each able to deliver very different flavours to its two different mash bills. So the yeasts in Kentucky do most certainly help to define the individuality of all bourbons. Each mash also contains backset (see sour mash below) but the exact quantity will vary according to the choice of each distiller.

After fermentation, and to continue to draw as much character as possible from the grain, the liquid wash and the fermented grain, looking like watery porridge, are entered together into the first still. The spirit exits the first still, a small column, at around 55% ABV. The condensed vapours or the vapours themselves then flow into a pot still called a doubler. If the vapours cross straight into the second still, that still is called a thumper, because of the noise created by the vapours rising through the water. During the second distillation alcoholic strength rises but only to around 60% ABV; by law, after the second distillation, the level of alcohol must not exceed 80% ABV to ensure the character of the grains is retained.

All colouring and flavouring must result only from the natural processes of fermentation, distillation and maturation. Nothing can be added to increase sweetness, to enhance flavour or to alter colour.

Spirit must then be matured in new, charred oak barrels. This process of burning the wood transforms carbohydrates into caramelized sugars and the heat draws these sugars, vanillin and colour towards the surface to form a reddish layer of sap behind the char, full of sweet flavours.

The habit of using new wood quite probably resulted from the early shipments downriver to New Orleans on boats that were unable to make the return trip. New barrels had to be made for each shipment and, in time, the taste for what was shipped in new wood must have become the preference. Certainly references to old Orleans or to old Ohio whiskey being red can be found in writings from the 1840s and in the novel *Moby Dick*, published in 1851, whale blood is compared to certain whiskeys of the day. Only whiskeys aged in new wood could absorb such levels of colour.

The spirit must barrel in new wood at less than 62.5% ABV. Most barrel at much less because the higher the strength in the barrel the more quickly character is drawn from the wood to the detriment of the finished whiskey. This is a particular risk in Kentucky where climatic conditions cause the alcohol strength to rise in the barrel whereas elsewhere alcohol strength tends to fall. Using new wood also means the character drawn from the wood is strong and aggressive and, coupled with the relatively small barrel size of only 200 litres, this means that the wood can contribute up to two thirds of bourbon's overall aroma and taste, or even more in older bourbons. The use of new wood and small barrels are reasons why bourbons spend fewer years in wood than scotch. The wood used is Quercus alba or American white oak. It's plentiful in the region and low in tannins but high in the vanillin and sugars that combine with the sweetness of the corn to generate much of the distinctively sweet character of bourbon.

The whiskey must be aged with no topping up for at least two years. Though, in reality, all are aged for a minimum of four years. Ageing is less critical than in Scotland because the local climate is hot and heat speeds up maturation. Summer temperatures can rise to 40°C and even higher in the warehouses, while winters are cold. In the summer, temperatures can also vary significantly between day and night, causing the wood to expand and contract constantly and forcing the spirit in and out of the pores to accelerate the maturation process. Six years in Kentucky are considered equal to nearer twenty in Scotland.

Kentucky is the only state allowed to put its name on the label and only if maturation takes place in Kentucky.

CHAR

While oak barrels are almost always toasted to enable the staves to be bent, bourbon barrels are charred, meaning they are subjected to much more intense heat. The level of flaming varies from level 1, representing a char similar to burnt toast to level 4, known as 'alligator' char. Most barrels receive a level 3 char that is typically around 3 mm thick. Heat partially caramelizes the hemicellulose and breaks down the lignin into vanillin. The char opens up the pores on the surface of the wood, giving the spirit greater opportunity to penetrate, extract and absorb the flavour compounds and colours from the wood as temperatures rise and fall. The layer of carbon in the char will also act as a filter, absorbing some of the less desirable elements and eliminating these, so softening the raw nature of the new-make spirit.

DEFINITIONS OF SPECIALTY BOURBONS

If bourbon is the appellation wine of American whiskeys, then single-barrel and small-batch are the grand crus. They show, very clearly that, when aged, American whiskeys can be much more varied and complex than their reputation to date might suggest. Their colour can be deep and their aromas and tastes rich and intense because character from the grain is retained during distillation and because the hot local climate stimulates interaction between the spirit and the new charred wood that is low in tannins but full of caramel and vanillin.

Small-batch

Maker's Mark was the first to produce such a whiskey in the 1950s. The distillery continues to only produce in small batches, choosing to make a little and have it all turn out right rather than to select the best. The term small-batch, however, was created by the Jim Beam

Company who described its small-batch productions as 'rare and exceptional bourbons married from a cross-section of barrels in the rack house'. A batch, in these circumstances, is much less than those used for everyday bottling but no maximum quantity has yet been defined. The whiskey is sourced from the same mash as its mother brand but aged longer and usually bottled at higher strengths to intensify the flavours.

Single barrel

'Cask' is the usual term in Scotland but, in Kentucky, it is 'barrel'. Blanton's was the first to be bottled and marketed as a 'single barrel', the product of just one barrel, usually carrying a detailed and hand-written specification on the label. These whiskeys are usually selected early and aged separately from other whiskeys where the distiller feels a certain taste profile can best be achieved. Whiskeys selected and bottled from different barrels will taste similar but they can and often do vary in their individual taste and alcoholic strength.

Vintage

These are distilled in a specific year with the year usually stated on the label and bottled only when the master distiller believes the whiskey to be at its best. They are chosen only as and when maturation reveals their special qualities. As their development ceases the whiskey is bottled and it is usual to specify the date of bottling on the label so the effective age of the whiskey is known.

OTHER AMERICAN WHISKEYS

Straight rye whiskey

Rye is a grain, introduced from Europe. It was widely used by the early settlers, not least because it proved to be easier to grow than barley. As the Whiskey Rebellion encouraged early distillers to trek west, inland from their initial settlements on the coast, their rye whiskey became a significant product in the states of Pennsylvania and Maryland.

On his Mount Vernon plantation, George Washington produced a whiskey from a mash bill that would be defined today as rye whiskey. At the time, his distillery was one of the largest in the country and, until Prohibition, the rye style remained the most popular whiskey in America. After Prohibition, however, American tastes had moved towards the softer Canadian style and rye whiskey never recovered.

To be called straight rye the mash must contain at least 51% rye grain. In all other circumstances it must conform to the regulations laid down for straight whiskey. The complex taste of rye whiskey is full of flavours that pepper the palate and few other whiskies can match its long finish except, perhaps, the peaty whiskies of Islay.

Straight corn whiskey

Corn was the native grain distilled by the early pioneers in Kentucky. It became known as the whiskey of the west. Today corn whiskey is made by Heaven Hill and some micro-distillers from a fermented mash of at least 80% corn, distilled to less than 80% ABV. It is usually un-aged or aged for only a short time in used or new oak barrels that have not been charred. A famed North Carolina moonshiner, Quill Rose, responded to a judge when asked to clarify the benefits of ageing with the words, 'your honour has been misinformed. I kept some for a week one time and I could not tell it was a bit better than when it was new and fresh.' The whiskeys, almost crystal clear like moonshine, usually lack the smooth and mellow character of aged whiskeys.

Straight wheat whiskey

Heaven Hill introduced this category with Bernheim Original Straight Wheat Whiskey. It is distilled from a mash, containing 51% wheat, 39% corn and 10% barley malt, to deliver a soft, mellow, fruity palate with gentle vanilla notes.

Kentucky whiskey

Whiskey aged in refill barrels is not eligible to be called straight bourbon whiskey. It can only be called Kentucky whiskey.

Tennessee whiskey

Whiskey distilling in Tennessee can be traced back at least to the eighteenth century and, even in the late nineteenth century, around 700 stills remained in operation. However, Prohibition took root in Tennessee in 1910 and lasted until 1938. Today only two distilleries operate legally, Jack Daniel's at Lynchburg and George Dickel in Cascade Hollow, less than twenty miles away in Tullahoma. George Dickel labels its Tennessee whisky without an 'e'.

In Lynchburg, there is no chance of sampling Jack Daniel's as the town and distillery remain dry. A referendum is all that is required to change the situation but the problem is that 25,000 people need to vote for change while the current population of Lynchburg is scarcely 400.

All regulations that govern the making of straight bourbon whiskey apply to straight Tennessee whiskey except the following, recognized in law since 1941, as being peculiar to Tennessee whiskey:

- The whiskey must be distilled in Tennessee, home of the Cherokee Indians and colonized by the Irish, rather than the Scots.

- The whiskey used to have to be distilled from a mash of at least 51% of any single grain but since August 2013 that grain has to be corn. So all Tennessee whiskey is distilled from corn using a grain formula similar to those used for traditional bourbons but with a relatively low percentage of rye.

- Prior to entering barrels for ageing, the spirit must be filtered through wood charcoal made from the sugar maple trees that grow in the area. The Jack Daniel's new-make spirit is dripped through columns three metres tall and packed with charcoal, a method of charcoal filtration, known as the Lincoln County process. If not invented by Alfred Eaton, he is known to have used this process in the 1820s in the distillery, located at Cave Springs on the outskirts of Lynchburg, which Jack Daniel was later to lease. At George Dickel the spirit is chill-filtered before resting in vats containing the charcoal. The process takes many days to soften the astringent new-make spirit and, during this time, a slightly sooty character is absorbed by the spirit, to add extra complexity to what would otherwise be a corn-fat whiskey. The Lincoln County process is what secures for Tennessee whiskey the status it has enjoyed since 1942, distinct from all other American whiskeys.

The spirit that exits this charcoal should not be confused with the tasteless spirit that exits charcoal filtration to become vodka. Considerable taste remains because of the high flavour grains used in the mash and the low level of alcohol at which the spirit leaves the still and enters the filtration column.

Single malts

Until recently virtually no single malt whiskeys were distilled in America or Canada. But today there are a number of micro-distilleries experimenting with malted barley, rye and sometimes corn and the number of single malts produced in America is likely to grow.

OTHER TERMS FOUND ON LABELS

Whiskey or whisky

In America both are legitimate spellings. In the nineteenth century, as the pioneer distillers developed America's native spirit, the imported whiskey with which they were familiar was Irish. Irish was the world's best selling whiskey and it was spelt with an 'e'. So 'whiskey' was simply understood to be the correct spelling. Towards the end of that century and particularly after Prohibition Scotch Whisky, spelt without the 'e', replaced Irish as the world's best seller and some distillers chose to adopt this spelling to encourage recognition for their brand, more as a whisky of the world than exclusively a whiskey of America.

Bottled in bond

This phrase signifies that a whiskey must be the product of one distillation season at one distillery and it must be aged for at least three years before being bottled at 100 proof or above.

Sour mash

Born in Scotland, in 1789, Dr James Crow is credited with perfecting the sour mash process in the 1830s. He worked as the distiller at the Old Oscar Pepper Distillery, now called Labrot & Graham and home today of Woodford Reserve. In the sour mash process a measure of backset, the residue or spent mash from the foot of the still after a previous distillation, is taken and added to the next mash in the fermenter. This raises the pH level, helps to acidify the otherwise alkaline mash and creates a stable medium in which the yeast can convert sugars into alcohol. The process also protects the mash from the risk of bacterial spoilage and gives continuity of style to each batch of bourbon, but at a cost. The greater the level of sour mash added to the mash in the fermenter, the less sugar is available for the yeast to convert into alcohol and the congeners that impact on flavour. Almost all American straight whiskey is made by the sour mash process and state as such on their labels. Sour mash does not refer to the taste of the whiskey.

MATURATION

You cannot make a bad whiskey good by ageing but you can certainly make a good whiskey better, or worse, and in Kentucky and Tennessee the extremes of summer and winter temperatures can also mean you lose a considerable quantity of whiskey during maturation. After six years a quarter of the whiskey could well have evaporated, two or three times more than in Scotland.

The climate and use of new wood combine to ensure that bourbon and Tennessee whiskeys also absorb exceptional levels of character during a relatively short time in wood. In fact, American whiskeys rarely state their age unless the whiskey is bottled as single-barrel or small-batch, when age may be a feature in their marketing. In these circumstances, maturation requires careful attention to the location of barrels in the warehouses. These can be up to nine storeys high and the heat rising in these warehouses can result in too much character being drawn from the new wood, overpowering other flavours and unbalancing the nature of the whiskey in later years. Producers can place barrels in particular areas of the warehouse to achieve certain results or gradually move barrels from the top to the bottom floors. Others blend a selection of barrels to maintain consistency or age whiskeys on the middle floors if intended for bottling as single barrels.

Each warehouse is individual: some built of brick, others from stone and some clad in iron shells. Some distillers heat their warehouses in winter. Their height provides different microclimates on every floor, though one distillery in Kentucky, Four Roses, and one in Tennessee, George Dickel, store their whiskeys in single-storey warehouses, believing that their more even cycles permit delivery of greater consistency and balance. However the warehouses are arranged, maturation has as much influence on taste and flavour in Kentucky and Tennessee as the whiskey's mash bill.

Quiz on American whiskey

1. In what year did an Act of Congress declare bourbon to be 'America's native spirit'?

   A. 1948
   B. 1955
   C. 1964
   D. 1972

2. Which grain must represent at least 51% of a bourbon whiskey mash?

   A. Corn
   B. Rye
   C. Barley
   D. Wheat

3. Which grain provides bourbon's characteristic spicy bite?

   A. Corn
   B. Rye

C. Barley

D. Wheat

4. What in Kentucky is free of irons and rich in calcium that makes the area so ideal for making whiskey?

A. Peat from Blue Mountains

B. Water from the Ohio River

C. Bog in the Pine Mountain area

D. Water filtered through limestone

5. What must not be used to enhance the character of a straight bourbon?

A. Flavourings

B. Colourings

C. Sweeteners

D. All of these

6. Which of these combinations of spirits best describes a typical American blended whiskey?

A. A blend of aged neutral grain spirit

B. Corn and straight bourbon whiskeys

C. Neutral grain spirit and bourbon whiskeys

D. Bourbon and rye whiskeys

7. To be classified as a 'straight whisk(e)y' in America a spirit must exit the still below what level of alcohol?

A. 72% ABV

B. 80% ABV

C. 90% ABV

D. 94% ABV

8. Which of these statements best describes how straight bourbon must be matured?

A. In new, charred oak barrels

B. In charred barrels

C. In new barrels

D. In oak barrels

9. In production of bourbon the term 'alligator' refers to what?

A. The depth of char

B. The fresh spring water

C. The spirit off the still

D. The distillery guard

10. The earliest barrels of whiskey were shipped from Limestone in Kentucky to where?

A. New Orleans

B. New York

C. Boston

D. Washington

11. Which grain was used to produce America's first whiskey?

A. Corn

B. Rye

C. Bourbon

D. Blended

12. Which of these whisk(e)ys is made using the Lincoln County process?

A. Maker's Mark

B. Jim Beam

C. Wild Turkey

D. Jack Daniel's

13. Who is recognized to have perfected the sour mash process?

A. Oscar Pepper

B. Jimmy Russell

C. James Crow

D. Bill Samuels

14. Who distilled whiskey at Mount Vernon?

A. Jim Beam
B. George Washington
C. Elijah Pepper
D. Evan Williams

15. What is the term used to describe raw spirit off the still in Kentucky and Tennessee?

A. Alligator
B. Moonshine
C. White Dog
D. Proof Spirit

MAKING COCKTAILS WITH AMERICAN WHISK(E)Y

Although the first mixed drink was probably made just after patrons of a tavern or inn realized that there was more than one bottle on the bar, the cocktail is an American invention and, in a neat case of serendipity, it just so happens that the whisk(e)ys of the USA are perfect mixing ingredients. New charred barrels contribute lots of sweet aromatics to bolster the corn and the small grains provide spice and interest without the taint of smokiness.

The Old-Fashioned

Although theoretically invented in the Pendennis club in Louisville, Kentucky the idea of an Old-Fashioned is a natural response to strident strong alcohol of all types.

Take a strong barrel proof spirit, often unpalatable at this level of alcohol and dilute it while chilling with ice to provide a more pleasing level of sweetness, to smooth the palate and to intensify the vanilla notes inherent in the whiskey. Add flavour, either by using fruits or aromatic bitters (or both). Add citrus oils from the fruit or zest to improve the aroma and you have almost the perfect cocktail.

The Old-Fashioned is one of the drinks that best demonstrate the evolution of the cocktail. Spirits continually improve in quality, distillers perfect their craft, farmers cultivate and produce raw materials ever better suited to producing spirit and the technology used in distillation is continually advancing. These better quality raw materials first lessen the need to mask deficiencies in the ingredients and eventually may well lead to changes not only in the quantities used in a recipe but in the ingredients themselves. The Pendennis recipe calls for slices of orange and cocktail cherries to be crushed in the preparation of the drink, a perfect response to whiskey of variable quality. Now bartenders around the world tend to omit them as the flavour of the whiskey needs polishing not masking.

As well as ingredients changing, the drinkers' palates change too. From infancy we all crave sweetness as it indicates ripeness in fruit. As our individual palates develop we accept more challenging flavours, almost always due to exposure to them in a positive setting. For example, the expansion of the high quality cocktail market has led to a change in palates in general, with deeper appreciation of sour and even bitter flavours in particular. This in turn has reduced the need for sugar in an Old-Fashioned.

When making an Old-Fashioned, it is important to remember that it is easy to add more modifying ingredients but impossible to take them out. Start off with minimal quantities of sugar and bitters and add more to taste.

The Modern Old-Fashioned

50ml American whiskey
5ml simple syrup (see page 95)
2 dashes Angostura or other aromatic bitters

Pour a quarter of the whiskey, along with the syrup and the bitters into a rocks glass with a couple of large cubes of ice and stir quite vigorously. This initial stirring will deliver much of the dilution of the drink. If you attempt to stir with a full glass of ice from the beginning the drink will take much longer to make. At intervals add portions of more whiskey and ice and continue to stir. In a 9oz rocks glass the drink will be ready when the liquid approaches the rim. Express the oils from a large orange twist, with all of the bitter pith removed, and use it to garnish the glass. Serve with a stir stick.

The last type of evolution evident in this most Darwinian of drinks is the changes that occur while drinking. The change over time in dilution, from just too strong to almost whiskey-flavoured water is one of the most enjoyable journeys in drinking and makes the stir stick an absolute necessity.

Old-Fashioneds work not just with any style of whiskey but with all aged spirits. Just adjust the quantity of sugar and type of bitters to find your favourite(s).

The Manhattan

Vermouth arrived on the shores of the USA in the latter half of the eighteenth century and was an immediate hit. Aromatized wines were originally consumed as an aperitif, neat or with a little ice in the old world, but on their arrival in America they were co-opted as cocktail modifiers. Their level of alcohol allowed for the tempering of strong spirits and their delicate vinous nature and herbaceous tones brought extra dimensions to the standard recipes of the time.

Of all the pairings and ménages-a-trois that vermouth was thrown into, one drink stands head and shoulders above the rest – the Manhattan. At its heart is the amazing affinity between rye whiskey and sweet vermouth. Versions that substitute dry styles in whole or in part are inferior.

40ml rye whiskey
20ml sweet vermouth
2 dashes Angostura Bitters

Stir all ingredients over ice in a large mixing glass and strain into a chilled 6oz cocktail glass. Garnish with a cocktail cherry and, for an extra lift to the aroma, an expressed then discarded orange twist.

The original recipe calls for a simple two parts rye whiskey to one part vermouth, which makes a delicious drink, particularly when using a lighter style of vermouth. It is worth experimenting with these proportions when using some of the more bitter varieties and if you choose to substitute rye with bourbon. Lurid pink cocktail cherries have no place in any drink, let alone this most adult of cocktails. Try preserving your own with your favourite whiskey and sugar when the cherries are in season and use them throughout the year

Using bourbon to make Manhattans produces a more relaxed style of drink and this has much to recommend it, not least the price of the ingredients. However, a spicy rye, ideally at 50% abv or more makes the very best Manhattan. Please experiment. The basic measures work with scotch (Rob Roy), aged rum (El Presidente) and cognac (Harvard).

Whiskey, raspberry, thyme and mint smash

One of the world's most famous American whiskey cocktails is the Mint Julep. Ubiquitous at the Kentucky Derby, this drink that grew out of the desire of plantation owners to show off their wealth, is in my opinion a profoundly flawed drink, lacking any kind of citrus bite to balance the sugar. Its cousin the Whiskey Smash is a far superior drink, using lemons and mint shaken with bourbon and served over crushed ice. This version goes even further. Bourbon has a natural affinity with both thyme and lemon thyme and a more surprising friendship with fresh sharp raspberries.

50ml bourbon
3 lemon wedges
3 sprigs thyme or lemon thyme
8 mint leaves
5 fresh raspberries
20ml simple syrup (see page 95)

Crush the mint, thyme and raspberries along with the lemon wedges in a metal shaker, taking care to thoroughly bruise the herbs to release their flavour and to extract the oils from the lemon zest. Add the other ingredients and shake hard, then strain over cracked or crushed ice in a large rocks glass or metal julep cup. Garnish with sprigs of mint and thyme and a fresh raspberry

Whiskey Smashes and variations tend to work better with softer styles of bourbon, particularly ones with wheat as one of the small grains; alternatively try this drink with a Tennessee whiskey.

14

CANADIAN WHISKY

HISTORICAL BACKGROUND

From the late nineteenth to the mid-twentieth century Canada was a very large producer of a particularly gentle style of whisky. Today, outside North America at least, sales of Canadian are small and, all too often, the whisky suffers from a lack of individual identity. Canadian regulations do not help much: they state: 'Canadian shall possess the aroma, taste and character generally attributed to Canadian whisky'.

The truth, however, is that Canada now offers a broad range of whiskies, some in the expected style and others that are increasingly able to challenge classic whiskies from elsewhere, and at competitive prices.

Canada was the destination of many Scots fleeing the Scottish Highlands in 1745 and the distilling skills they took to Canada were as good as any that went to America. The first still licence was issued in 1794 but early distillation used molasses which were readily available from the Caribbean, rather than grain. It was a brewer named Thomas Molson who, in 1821, distilled Canada's first whisky, followed later that century by many of the names that remain familiar today, including Hiram Walker and Joseph Seagram, both millers who wanted to profit from their excess grain.

Initially, the distilleries were all in eastern Canada, hugging the shores of the St Lawrence River. Seagram's was based in Waterloo, Ontario. Hiram Walker's distillery, now called Wiser's, remains in Windsor, Ontario at Canada's southernmost point, just across the Detroit River from the city of Detroit in Michigan. Only in the twentieth century were distilleries built in the prairies to the west, close to the extensive fields of wheat, barley and rye that are harvested in this region.

The arrival of Prohibition in America transformed Canadian whisky production into a large scale, high volume industry. Canada itself had tried prohibition in 1918 but it had lasted scarcely a year. It was unworkable, unenforceable and unpopular. A year later, Prohibition hit America and business boomed as Canadian distillers worked tirelessly and successfully to meet demand, transforming the waters that separated Detroit in America from Canada into busy highways. It was the theft, in 1929, of a shipment of Canadian whisky that was intended for Al Capone which led to one of Prohibition's most violent shootings, the Valentine's Day Massacre.

After Prohibition, memories of the heavier pre-Prohibition styles of whisky had faded and demand for the lighter whisky from Canada continued, prompting Canadian distillers to become totally wedded to high-tech, column-still production. Not for them a number of small distilleries making individual pot-still whiskies, instead production was consolidated to develop the means to make a vast range of whiskies under one roof, using different mash bills, different distillation strengths, varying quantities of 'base' and 'flavouring' whiskies and different woods. The Canadians also added other mature spirits or wines to their blends to create additional flavouring.

When demand slumped during the second half of the twentieth century the world was awash with Canadian whisky, causing serious and lasting damage to its reputation. The massive decline in sales left only America as a significant export market for this light style of whisky.

PRODUCTION

As in America, rum was the first alcohol to be produced in Canada. However, when it came to producing spirit from grain, even more so than in America, rye was found to be the grain most able to survive the bitter cold. Rye became the dominant grain used to make whisky, although using the term 'rye' to describe Canadian whisky today is, in most cases, a misnomer. Only a very few can claim to be true rye whiskies.

All Canadian whisky must be distilled in Canada. The vast majority are blends of up to fifty whiskies, each distilled from a mash that can use any grain and this is the reason why the mash bill usually defines much of the character of a Canadian whisky.

The malted barley is dried with clean heat, meaning Canadian whisky has none of the smoky flavour familiar in scotch. Most Canadian distillers use corn as the grain for their base spirit which is triple distilled in column stills to any strength, but usually to around 94%–95% ABV. This process removes many undesirable elements but much of the character as well. The resulting base spirit is clean and relatively neutral in character, accounting for a significant percentage of the fill of most Canadian blends, one reason why Canadian whiskies are recognized to be some of the lightest in the world.

To provide the flavouring whiskies demanded by the blenders and permitted by the limited regulations different yeasts are used, as are single and double distillations, in column and pot stills. The flavouring distillates are distilled separately to lower levels of alcohol to retain more character from the rye grain but still to above 70% ABV. Numerous cuts then allow many different styles of new-make spirit to be collected and stored for future blending. The percentage of flavouring whiskies included in standard blends is likely to be less than 20%. Certainly, an American straight rye or even a number of bourbons will include much more rye grain in the mash than a typical Canadian.

To create the brands, these different distillates can be blended prior to, during or after maturation, which must last a minimum of three years. Some new wood is used but, generally, the wood influence is limited as the ex-bourbon barrels widely used are refilled as many as six or seven times.

A maximum of 9.09% of the final product may consist of flavourings from another spirit (aged for a minimum of two years),

from wine with no age specification or from fruit concentrates. Standard blends usually have no additives whereas the older whiskies may well benefit from the addition of aged whiskies or brandies.

The resulting whisky is generally light on any character drawn from the grain or the wood, and is more the creation of innovative blenders. It is delicate and smooth with only hints of rye, highly mixable, definitely not simple but generally not complex either. Though Canadian whisky is usually sold as blends, a very small quantity of malts can now be found along with some exclusive hand-crafted pot-still whiskies, bottled as single rye or corn whiskies.

Canadian whisky is always spelt without an 'e'.

Quiz on Canadian whisky

1. Who distilled Canada's first whisky?

   A. Hiram Walker
   B. Thomas Molsen
   C. Joseph Seagram
   D. J.P. Wiser

2. Which grain is predominant in production of Canadian whisky?

   A. Rye
   B. Wheat
   C. Corn
   D. Barley

3. Who was inspired by a theft of Canadian whisky to commit a massacre?

   A. Al Capone
   B. Frank Costello
   C. Carlo Gambino
   D. Bugs Moran

4. Which of these flavourings are allowed as additions to Canadian whisky?

A. Fruit concentrates
B. Wine
C. Other spirits
D. All of these

15

JAPANESE WHISKY

The Japanese whisky industry started in 1923 when Masataka Taketsuru, who had studied whisky distilling in Scotland went, as master distiller, into partnership with Shinjiro Torii, who built Yamazaki: Japan's first distillery. In 1929, Japan's first whisky was launched and Torii's venture grew into the giant Suntory, now Japan's biggest whisky producer.

In 1933, Taketsuru left to found his own distillery in Yoichi, on Japan's cold northern island of Hokkaido where conditions are closer to those in Scotland. His company became Nikka. Today, with grain plants and malt distilleries at Yoichi and at Miyagikyo, north-east of Tokyo, Nikka is Japan's second largest distiller.

The Kirin Company also makes whisky in the foothills of Mount Fuji but many of the smaller distilleries either shut down after the Asian financial crisis in the nineties or turned to making shochu, leaving Suntory and Nikka to dominate whisky making in Japan.

Though its success remains very dependent on the home market, Japanese whisky is fast gaining an international reputation for individuality and awards now confirm its status, alongside the very best of the world's whiskies. The quality and variety of the whiskies that each distillery produces flow from the commitment the Japanese have made to an in-depth examination of the whole process of producing whisky and to their constant innovation at all levels of production.

As in Scotland, the market is dominated by blends but malt whiskies, initially created for the blends, are now being bottled as single and blended malts. Unlike in Scotland, however, where blenders buy and sell malts from nearly 100 individual distilleries to create their house styles, in Japan distilleries each produce for themselves the many different styles of malts they require. These producers use peated and unpeated barley malt; different yeasts and varied fermentation times; stills of different shapes and sizes, some even coal-fired; plus different cuts and many woods, including scented Japanese oak and plum liqueur casks, to give individuality and personality to each whisky.

The style of malts preferred by the Japanese is light, delicate, fragrant and low in cereal notes, an ideal combination of character for blends that the Japanese enjoy as refreshing drinks, drunk long with lots of ice. Rich and fruity whiskies can also be found, as can the much more robust smoky and peaty whiskies sourced particularly from the northern island of Hokkaido.

Quiz on Japanese whisky

1. Which of these statements best describes the style of whisky most preferred by the Japanese?

   A. Delicate and fragrant
   B. Smoky and peaty
   C. Heavy and robust
   D. Rich and fruity

2. What is the name of Japan's first distillery?

   A. Yoichi
   B. Yamazaki
   C. Hanyu
   D. Shinshu

1. A; 2. B

Answers

16

SCOTCH WHISKY

HISTORY

Though its origins are lost in the mists of time, the term whisky derives from the Gaelic *uisge beatha*, meaning 'water of life' and, for sure, whisky has been distilled in Scotland for centuries. The earliest reference can be traced to the Scottish Exchequer Rolls of 1494 to 1495: 'To Friar John Cor, by order of the King, to make aqua vitae VIII bolls of malt.'

The earliest mention of a distillery appears in 1690, though distillation in private houses was recorded before then and taxes on spirits were fixed as early as 1644. Following the 1707 Act of Union with England, more taxes were imposed but few were collected. The Scottish climate and water were ideal for growing the barley for whisky making and the Scottish highlands were equally ideal for making illicit whisky, hidden from the eyes of customs officers or other government officials. By the 1820s, hundreds of illegal stills were seized annually and most whisky was still being drunk, duty free, in Scotland. In 1823 the Excise Act was passed to sanction the distilling of whisky in return for payment of a licence fee of £10 along with further payments relating to production. This legislation proved to be the foundation of the Scotch whisky industry we know today.

Flavoursome malts, produced in pot stills, were the style of whiskies produced at this time. Their heavy, strong, usually harsh and varied character tended to restrict their consumption to Scotland. There was no whisky industry as such and the whiskies produced lacked any consistency. Locals produced whisky for their own consumption or to share with neighbours.

It was the invention of the continuous still by Robert Stein in 1827 and the improvements made by Aeneas Coffey, who patented his design in 1831 that initiated the industry by making possible the mass production of grain whisky in large-scale licensed grain distilleries built in the Lowlands near the large cities of Glasgow and Edinburgh.

Andrew Usher pioneered blending the different malts to create more consistency and branding the whisky to generate more confidence when, in 1853, he introduced Usher's Old Vatted Glenlivet. Using experience and lessons learned from blending teas he, and numerous other Scottish merchants, then explored opportunities to blend the new lighter grain whiskies, produced in Coffey stills in the Lowlands with the malts, distilled in pots in the Highlands. They became known as the 'whisky barons' and their whisky blends, now lighter in character, were more suited to popular tastes. The timing of the arrival of these scotch blends could not have been more fortuitous. Until this time cognac and soda had been the drink of choice of those who ruled the world but, in the 1870s, vineyards in Cognac were destroyed by the phylloxera aphid. These new blends were ideally suited to take advantage of cognac's demise and, in the twenty years it took for cognac to recover, the Scottish blenders were able to develop a taste for scotch around the world. Better still, they were now able to replicate the skill of the cognac houses in producing a consistent product and branding their whiskies for ease of recognition.

Scotland has the highest concentration of distilleries in the world. It produces more different styles of whisky than any other country. Today, many distilleries market single malt whiskies to represent this variety and individuality. However, the majority of the new-make spirit from these single distilleries is used in the production of scotch blends, a use that by no means represents any dilution in their value.

The skill of the blenders is to take numerous single whiskies of differing ages and regions, maybe aged in different woods and to blend them in such a way that each of the whiskies complements and enhances the others. The resulting blends remain individual, but they deliver specific characteristics intended to appeal to defined tastes with absolute consistency. Blending is an art acquired by very few during years of experience and the blends they create account for well over 90% of all scotch sold in the world today.

Scotch whisky can only be made in Scotland where the natural elements of the water, peat and the Scottish climate, together with local tradition, combine to have a profound effect on flavour.

Those who make scotch exercise skills handed down from generation to generation. Their craft and their communities, dedicated to the production of whisky, ensure that scotch is an integral part of Scottish heritage and that Scotland is the world's leading centre for making whisky.

THE DEFINITION OF SCOTCH WHISKY

The Scotch Whisky Regulations 2009 define scotch as a whisky:

a) Which has been produced at a distillery in Scotland from water and malted barley to which only whole grains of other cereals may be added, all of which have been:

- processed at that distillery into a mash,

- converted at that distillery into a fermentable substrate only by endogenous enzyme systems and

- fermented at that distillery only by addition of yeast.

b) Which has been distilled to an alcoholic strength by volume of less than 94.8% so that the distillate has an aroma and taste derived from the raw materials used in, and the method of its production.

c) Which has been wholly matured in an excise warehouse in Scotland in oak casks of a capacity not exceeding seven hundred litres, the period of that maturation being not less than three years.

d) Which retains the colour, aroma and taste derived from the raw materials used in, and the method of its production and maturation, and to which no substance other than water and plain caramel colouring may be added.

The Scotch Whisky Act forbids, inter alia the production in Scotland of whisky other than scotch. It also prohibits producers to mature or to blend whiskies in Scotland other than scotch.

Both this act and the European Spirits Definition Regulation specify a minimum alcoholic strength of 40% alcohol by volume. This applies to all scotch whisky bottled and/or offered for sale within or exported from the European Community

WHAT IS NEW-MAKE SPIRIT?

A distillate fresh from the still may not be called whisky. It may only be called whisky after three years maturation in wood in Scotland. Until then it is called new make spirit. During fermentation the levels and the proportion of fragrant and fruity esters, of smoky phenols and leathery feints created will define the broad character of this distillate.

WHAT IS A MALT WHISKY?

Malt whisky is produced from only one grain, barley, water and yeast. Distillation is in batches, in pot stills, to around 70% ABV and the new-make spirit is aged in used oak casks. This was the style of whisky initially made and drunk predominantly in Scotland, the product of a pot still sited on an isolated farm rather than in a distillery and drunk raw, fresh off the still rather than aged in wood.

During the nineteenth and twentieth centuries, malts gained recognition beyond Scotland only as ingredients in blends but, since the 1960s, initiated by Glenfiddich, single scotch malts have gained significant recognition in their own right. Today, single malts are shipped for their own consumption from around ninety distilleries in Scotland while others are shipped to other countries for use in their own production of blends.

A single malt is the product of a single distillery whereas a blended malt scotch whisky is a blend of two or more single malts from different distilleries. Historically, a blend of malts was known as a 'vatted malt' but, since 2003 the term 'blended malt' has been the correct description. Also since 2003, the term 'pure malt' has been outlawed by the Scottish authorities.

WHAT IS A GRAIN WHISKY?

Scottish grain whisky is produced from a mash of malted barley and other unmalted cereals, either corn or wheat. These base cereals are pressure cooked to make their starch soluble and to begin the conversion process before the malt is added. In Scotland no artificial enzymes can be used to accelerate this conversion. The resulting sugary liquid, called the 'wort', is fermented to produce a wash. The wash is distilled in a column or Coffey still because this type of still produces large quantities of spirit more efficiently than the pot. The vapours are collected as they condense at between 90% and 94.8% ABV, to provide a distillate much lighter than the spirit collected from pot stills for malts. This 'new-make' grain spirit is filled into American oak casks, usually first-fill, and matured for at least three years. The spirit is light in character meaning that it ages relatively quickly.

By law, grain whisky must have 'an aroma and taste derived from the raw materials used in and the method of, its production'. So, even though it will be distilled to higher levels of alcohol than malts and generally be lighter in aroma and taste, matured grain whisky will develop a silky texture and luscious mouth feel and each of the five grain distilleries will produce their own individual style of whisky.

Grain whisky is used primarily for blending but some is bottled as grain whisky. Blended grain scotch whisky is a blend of two or more single grain scotch whiskies sourced from different distilleries.

WHAT IS A BLEND OF SCOTCH WHISKY?

The invention of the continuous still in the 1830s stimulated development of whisky blends, meaning blends of at least one single grain whisky from the column still and at least one single malt from a pot still. In practice, blends contain a number of distillates, each of which is separately entitled to the description Scotch whisky. Typically, the proportions will be 40% malt whisky to 60% grain but more malt will be used in deluxe blends and less in some standard blends. The age of a blend must be defined by the youngest spirit in that blend.

Blends initiated the concept of branding Scotch whisky because the skills of the blender could create house style whiskies to match defined consumer tastes and needs in different countries and climates. The key was to achieve absolute consistency even when using individual casks that differ from year to year or even disappear and need to be replaced.

Blends account for more than 90% of all the scotch that's sold in the world.

MAKING MALT WHISKY

Barley, yeast and Scottish water are the basic raw materials for Scotch malt whisky. Any cereal grain may be malted to make whiskey. But, in scotch, the malt will always be malted barley. Distillers can choose from many varieties of barley and choice will depend on cost, alcohol yield and disease resistance. Chariot, Golden Promise and Optic have all been favourites in the last fifty years, but whether any contributes distinctive aromatics or flavours to a whisky is not proven.

MALTING

Malting prepares starches in the grains for conversion by activating enzymes that will stimulate germination. A few distilleries retain their own floor maltings. But today most distilleries will buy in their malt, to agreed specifications, from large independent maltings.

Floor maltings

Barley is first steeped (soaked) in warm water for up to two days. Once drained from the steeping tanks, the wet and warm malt is spread out on a stone or cement floor to germinate for five to six days. Natural enzymes are activated to break down the starch cell walls and convert the starch held in the endosperm of the grain into sugars to feed the growing shoots.

The barley begins to grow shoots and, at this point, it is called 'green malt'. The objective of this exercise is only to activate these enzymes and not to convert all the starch into the sugar required to feed the growth of the shoots. So the green malt will be turned regularly to control the rate of germination, a process that will also stop the developing rootlets from matting together.

Drum maltings

Here the saturated barley is transferred into large drums and cool, humid air is blown through them to control temperatures. Occasionally these drums are rotated to prevent the rootlets from matting together.

KILNING

Whichever malting process is used kilning arrests germination by drying the green malt when the growing rootlets are around three quarters the length of the grain. Kilning, which lasts around thirty hours, is the process of blowing hot air through a perforated floor over which the green malt has been spread. This stops the conversion process and enables the malt to be held without loss of quality until required for mashing. The moisture content is reduced to around 5% making it possible for the malt to be ground in a mill. If desired, kilning can be used to impregnate the grains with smoky flavours by burning peat turf in the oven beneath.

PEAT

In waterlogged bogs, plants are unable to rot. Instead one layer of vegetation becomes compressed under another and transforms into acidic, decayed vegetation known as peat. Traditionally, this has been cut and dried to provide a cheap fuel for those who live where few other natural resources exist. When burned, the peat releases smoke full of strong aromas, or phenols, and these cling to the exterior of the grain. As the nature of the peat varies from area to area, so the character the smoke imparts to the grain varies according to where the peat is cut. Lowland malt contains more vegetable matter. Highland malt contains moss and heather. Malt cut by the sea is saturated with salt and may contain seaweed.

Distillers will specify to maltsters the levels of peating they require:

- Lightly peated = 1–5 ppm of total phenols

- Medium peated = 10–20 ppm

- Heavily peated = 30–50 ppm

The amount of peating is measured by the concentration of phenolic compounds in the smoke, not in the whisky.

MALT HOUSE

After kilning the dressing machine removes unwanted rootlets (malt culms) and the malt is stored in the malt house until required for mashing.

Milling

The dressed barley malt is now milled into a coarse flour, called grist, that is suitable for mashing.

Mashing in the mash house

Mashing extracts soluble sugars from the starch remaining in the malted barley grist, a process that takes up to ten hours.

Grist is mixed with hot water and run into a mash tun to promote the enzyme activity required to complete conversion of the starches into fermentable sugars. When whiskies other than malts are to be made, unmalted grains may be combined with the malted barley at this stage.

The mash is stirred and the resulting sugary wort is drained off through perforations in the bottom of the mash tun. The process is repeated twice and each time water is added at higher temperatures, to wash out as much sugar as possible. Wort from the second addition of water is sent to a fermenting vessel. Wort from the third is combined with the first water and used in the next mash. The wort flows into a holding vessel called the 'underback', where it cools to temperatures ideal for fermentation.

The 'draff' or spent grains left in the mash tun are removed and usually sold as cattle feed.

FERMENTATION IN THE TUN ROOM

The cooled wort is poured into a 'washback', which may be made from wood or stainless steel.

All scotch distillers use the same strain of yeast to convert sugars into alcohol, carbon dioxide and the flavour compounds, known as congeners. Fermentation can be short and completed in less than forty-eight hours or it can take longer. A short fermentation will tend to result in a more malty character whereas a longer one will generate more complex and fruity flavours.

The fermented liquid, called 'wash', is less than 10% ABV, but full of flavourful and aromatic compounds for distillation to concentrate.

DISTILLING USING THE POT STILL

Malt whisky is always produced in batches in pot stills and the stills are always made of copper. The shape and size of these stills have a significant influence on the character of individual malt whiskies. A tall still tends to produce lighter spirits as only the more volatile, fragrant and fruity alcohols can climb the neck and pass over into the condenser. Glenmorangie stills, for example, are more than five metres tall. Stills with short necks tend to produce a richer, oilier spirit because heavier vapours are able to pass over into the lyne arm and down into the condenser rather than condensing sooner and falling back into the still as reflux. Malt whisky is produced by at least two distillations. The first, in a wash still, shapes the character of the new-make spirit and the second, in a low wines or spirit still, refines it.

Heating, usually by steam-filled heaters, causes the alcohol and other volatile compounds, known as congeners, to vaporize and to pass up the neck of the still. As the vapours cool they condense back into liquid, containing a higher percentage of alcohol called 'low wines'. The congeners created during fermentation and held in these vapours give malt whisky its core character.

The residue from the first distillation, called 'pot ale' or 'spent wash' is removed for sale, like the draff, to farmers.

The low wines retained from this first distillation are now entered into the smaller spirits still and from here the flow of spirit is separated into three parts. The so-called middle cut or heart usually exits the still between 75% and 65% ABV. Alcohols collected before the middle cut, called foreshots or esters, are more fragrant and fruity whereas alcohols collected after, called feints or fusel oils are heavier and more oily. The middle cut is retained for maturation except on the rare occasion when a third distillation takes place. Then some of the esters and/or feints may be retained as well, depending precisely on where the distiller chooses to make the cuts. Where these cuts are made is key to flavour. The remaining distillate is mixed with the next batch of low wines and redistilled.

The new-make spirit, collected for maturation, is directed into the spirit receiver, transferred to a holding tank, reduced to around 63% ABV and piped into oak casks to mature into whisky.

Copper

Stills are manufactured from copper because copper does not react unfavourably with alcohol. It's also a good conductor of heat, malleable and so easy to shape. Contact, or conversation, with copper extracts and retains from the wash some of the heavier and less attractive compounds like sulphur, which is converted into copper sulphate. This conversation means that the height and shape of the still are critical to the flavour and style of the final spirit. A rule of thumb is that the taller the still, the longer the conversation and so the lighter the spirit. The shorter and more squat the shape of the still, the shorter the conversation and the heavier the spirit.

Over time the copper walls will wear thin and panels will need to be replaced.

Condensing

Vapours condense either in shell-and-tube condensers in which coils of copper pipes filled with cold water cool and condense the vapours or in traditional worm tubs where a coiled pipe containing the hot vapours is immersed in a tank of cold water. The latter reduces the amount of copper contact and so tends to contribute towards the production of heavier, oilier spirits.

ESTERS AND FEINTS

These are the two distinct compounds to be found in a new-make spirit. Esters are the fruity, fragrant characteristics found in higher alcohols and they decline as strength drops during the distillation process. Some are not beneficial and so they are removed with the first fraction of distillate. Others are retained along with the middle cut or heart, to give whisky much of its character. Additional esters may be created during the maturation process as the alcohols interact with each other and with the wood.

Feints appear later and can be collected at levels of alcohol as low as 57% ABV because some of the oily compounds held in the feints can add texture and flavour to a whisky but collection will cease before other compounds appear that will be detrimental to aroma and flavour.

In a new-make spirit the distiller's aim is for the esters and feints to be in balance.

MATURATION

Until the end of the nineteenth century most whisky was sold straight from the still. But since 1915, the law has required that all whiskies sold in the UK must have been aged in oak casks for at least three years and all whisky, to be sold as scotch, must be matured in oak casks in Scotland.

Oak is water tight yet porous, so while casks do not leak, they do absorb oxygen. Casks breathe, pulling spirit into the pores, precipitating an interchange with the colour and flavour compounds in the wood. The porosity also allows the contents to evaporate at an initial rate of around 2% per annum. Evaporation includes water and alcohol and, as the alcoholic strength declines, the rate of evaporation will slow down. Initially, a layer of carbon on the surface of a toasted or charred cask helps to remove immature notes in the raw new-make spirit and, because oak is permeable, air also helps to mellow the spirit through oxidation.

Oak is free from strong odours and resins but different oaks do contain varying levels of tannins and other beneficial flavour compounds. As the liquid expands in warmer weather and contracts when colder, the spirit penetrates and exits the pores in the wood, drawing additional texture, flavours and aromas into the spirit and increasing the whisky's overall levels of complexity.

Casks must have a capacity of less than 700 litres to ensure ample opportunity for interaction between spirit and wood. The smaller the cask, the greater the surface area contact with the spirit and so the greater the influence of the wood.

Scotch is aged in wood that has already been used to age other spirits or wines. The residue left in the wood from these initial fills and the nature of the wood itself make different contributions to a new-make spirit but the level of contribution does depend on how many times the cask has been refilled. A cask filled with new-make spirit for the first time is referred to as first fill, for a second time, second fill and so on. Each fill reduces the wood's yield and influence, permitting a distiller to choose a combination best suited to any particular new make-spirit and appropriate to the level of oak influence required in the finished whisky. A second fill ex-bourbon cask could yield as little as 25% of the character drawn from a first fill and a third fill, as little as 10%. A second fill ex-sherry cask could yield as little as 50% and a third fill, perhaps no more than 15%.

Distillers predominantly use two types of cask, some as shipped, others broken down and reassembled to create casks of different sizes. Some may use only one type of cask. Others may use two or more, intending each to impart its individuality to the new-make spirit.

- Ex-sherry casks, made from toasted European oak, have an open, porous grain and contain a significant level of tannins. These contribute lots of dark colour and structure plus aromas reminiscent of a rich fruit and nut cake. Traditionally, sherry was shipped to the UK in cask and so provided ample supplies of empty casks. Declining demand for sherry and local bottling in Spain reduced availability and increased costs so that these are now the choice of a minority of distillers.

- Ex-bourbon barrels, made from charred American white oak have a tighter grain and are low in tannins and high in vanillin and lactones. These contribute a lighter, amber colour plus aromas of vanilla and coconut as well as hints of spices like cinnamon. These barrels are readily available to scotch producers and they are used by most distilleries because the bourbon distillers in America can only use the barrels once.

- Ex-port, madeira, rum and some ex-wine casks are also used, particularly for finishing.

Maturation provides opportunities to use different woods with different original fills. Some may be charred and others toasted to draw more or less character from the wood. Different sizes also provide varying levels of potential contact between the wood and the spirit and different ages vary the wood's level of influence. The possible permutations are limitless. Depending on the wood, as well as time in cask and climate, the overall influence can be very significant, accounting for as much as 70% of the final flavour in a bottled scotch.

FINISHING

Wood finishes were pioneered by Glenmorangie in the 1990s. To 'finish' means to transfer whisky matured in ex-bourbon casks into active casks previously used for maturing wines, fortified wines or other spirits for a short period of secondary maturation. This provides an additional level of flavour, intended to enhance and enrich the overall character of a whisky.

Blending

Most scotch is sold as blends, containing grain whiskies and numerous malts blended together to marry the different flavours, aromas and textures to match specific market tastes and to maintain the profiles of well-known, existing brands.

Over time, as distilleries close and open and climate change slows down or speeds up rates of maturation, different selections of whiskies may be required to maintain continuity. This is why blends are not the result of recipes that specify the whiskies and the quantities to be used but selections, made by the blender to consistently achieve a desired character. At any time, circumstances may oblige a blender to choose different whiskies to maintain consistency. Once blended the whisky may be returned to cask to 'marry'.

Any age statement on a blend must refer to the youngest whisky in the blend.

Marrying

Prior to bottling the contents of a number of individual casks will be combined in a wood or stainless steel vat to marry. The married whiskies may then be returned to other casks for a further period of maturation before bottling.

Addition of caramel

Spirit caramel may be added to maintain a consistent colour.

Bottling and chill filtration

During maturation, evaporation in cask will usually reduce the alcohol percentage to between 50% and 60% ABV. Some bottlings are released at cask strength, meaning bottled at the alcohol percentage by volume of the whisky when the cask was emptied. However most Scotch whisky is bottled at or around the minimum of 40% ABV, so most are reduced with water to the desired bottling strength.

After reduction the whiskies still contain the fatty acids formed during fermentation. These compounds are tasteless but, when the whisky is further diluted to drink, or if it is subject to cold temperatures, these compounds may precipitate and cause the whisky to become hazy and less attractive. To ensure a whisky retains its clarity, chill filtering prior to bottling reduces the temperature of the liquid sufficiently for these fatty acids as well as some proteins and esters to precipitate and be filtered out and removed. This process will ensure the whisky remains crystal clear but removal of these compounds is also likely to reduce some of the mouth feel and to eliminate some of the flavour compounds.

REGIONALITY

Whiskies made and matured in one region can share certain characteristics, but this is more because of familiar production methods and for historical and stylistic reasons than because of terroir. The geographical boundaries, though legally defined, owe their existence more to politics than to any similarities in taste of the whiskies produced within each region. What's more, whiskies today are often distilled, matured and diluted for bottling in different locations so any geographical classification has even less significance. All that is certain is that the individuality of each whisky does owe much to its distillery though probably more to the people who work there and to the decisions they take than to the distillery's location.

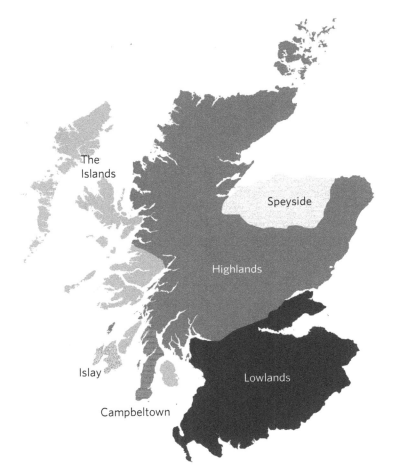

Map of the classified Scottish whisky production regions

Lowlands Here, there are only three distilleries producing single malts but it must not be forgotten that the bulk of grain whisky, is produced in this region. The individual malts are generally light in weight, unpeated or very lightly peated. Apart from this, the whiskies here can and do vary in character from fragrant and grassy to malty and dry.

Highlands This, the largest of regions, stretches from Loch Lomond in the south to the northernmost point of Scotland, excepting only the area of Speyside. The region produces an enormous variety of whiskies, from the predominantly fruity and spicy whiskies in the north and central Highlands, to the often fragrant and floral, lighter whiskies of the south; from the fruity and spicy whiskies in the west to the varied and complex whiskies of the east

Speyside The river Spey flows 100 miles from south of Loch Ness past Aviemore, into the Moray Firth to the north. The rugged area surrounding its lower reaches boasts around fifty distilleries, the world's largest concentration of individual distilleries. The character of the modern scotch industry originated here and it remains the home of complex and elegant whiskies with great finesse, some light and floral, others richer and fruitier. Many will be found at the heart of the blends.

Islands This is a disparate region comprising the very different islands of Arran, Jura, Mull, Skye and the Orkneys. Peat is a common, though by no means exclusive, thread between them and the whiskies remain as individual as the islands themselves.

Islay This small western isle forms its own whisky region and, situated just across the sea from Ireland, it is quite possibly where distillation arrived in Scotland. The island is renowned for its strong, robust and heavily peated malts, produced on its south coast. These are full of brine from the sea. The island also produces softer whiskies with mere hints of peat or with no peat at all. Though increasingly sipped on their own, malts from Islay are used extensively to add depth to many blends.

Campbeltown Situated to the south-east of Islay, this tip of land, stretching out into the Atlantic, boasted many distilleries in the 1880s and a thriving whisky business prior to Prohibition in the United States but today only three distilleries survive, producing pungent, full-bodied whiskies.

Quiz on Scotch whisky

1. In what year did an Excise Act lay the foundations of today's Scotch whisky industry?

    A. 1644
    B. 1707
    C. 1823
    D. 1827

2. Scotch blends account for what percentage of all scotch sold in the world today?

    A. Over 75%
    B. Over 80%
    C. Over 85%
    D. Over 90%

3. A mash for scotch may be distilled to what maximum level of alcohol?

    A. 72% ABV
    B. 84.5% ABV
    C. 94.8% ABV
    D. 96.4% ABV

4. Which grain(s) are permitted in the production of scotch malt whisky?

    A. Barley
    B. Rye
    C. Corn
    D. All of these grains

5. Single malts, bottled as such, gained global recognition in their own right from which decade?

    A. 1880s
    B. 1900s
    C. 1930s

D. 1960s

6. Which of these terms is a correct and legal description of a blend of malt whiskies?

A. A vatted malt
B. A blended malt
C. A pure malt
D. An individual malt

7. Which of these statements places, in the correct order, the liquids produced in making scotch?

A. Mash—wort—wash
B. Wort—mash—wash
C. Mash—wash—wort
D. Wash—mash—wort

8. Which of these statements places, in the correct order, the processes in making scotch?

A. Steeping—kilning—germination
B. Kilning—steeping—germination
C. Steeping—germination—kilning
D. Germination—steeping—kilning

9. Peat found in the Highlands typically contains what type of plant materials?

A. Vegetable
B. Seaweed
C. Fruit
D. Heather

10. What best describes the character of scotch if esters are retained during distillation?

A. Peaty
B. Fragrant

C. Oily

D. Earthy

11. What best describes the character of scotch if feints are retained during distillation?

A. Light

B. Sulphury

C. Oily

D. Fragrant

12. Worm tubs, where a coiled pipe containing hot vapours is immersed in a tank of cold water, will help to enhance what characteristics in a scotch?

A. Fruitiness

B. Aromatics

C. Peatiness

D. Texture

13. What is the maximum size of cask permitted for the maturation of scotch?

A. 600 litres

B. 700 litres

C. 800 litres

D. No restrictions

14. The chill-filtering process is used to enhance what characteristic of scotch?

A. Clarity

B. Dryness

C. Freshness

D. Texture

15. Which region in Scotland boasts the world's largest concentration of individual distilleries?

    A. Lowlands
    B. Speyside
    C. Highlands
    D. Islands

16. Which single malt pioneered the current popularity of single malts?

    A. Glenfiddich
    B. Glenmorangie
    C. Glen Grant
    D. Glen Scotia

17. In what year was a law passed requiring all scotch to be aged for at least three years?

    A. 1905
    B. 1910
    C. 1915
    D. 1920

MAKING COCKTAILS WITH SCOTCH WHISKY

Single malt whiskies are some of the finest expressions of the distiller's art no matter where in the world spirits are produced. The amount of skill required to balance all of the disparate influences on final flavour is incredible, from the type and treatment of the malt and choice of barrel to the selection of the final bottling proof to exhibit the spirit to best effect. Unfortunately for the bartender or home mixologist the wonderful aroma of smoke, inculcated in the whisky when the malt is drying over fires of peat is a very difficult characteristic to include in a cocktail. Either it must be used so sparingly as to make its inclusion pointless or used in quantity, leaving all other components overpowered.

This is referenced in most cocktail recipe books by the lack of classic Scotch whisky recipes, with most of the well known drinks having more familiar and usually tastier versions made with other spirits, such as the Rob Roy and Manhattan. The development of Scotch whisky cocktails has also been hampered by the insistence of the 'whisky connoisseur' that even the addition of ice is a cardinal sin.

Blended Scotch whisky is a better proposition for the cocktailian. The use of grain whisky as a smokeless base, and the inclusion of lighter malts in the blend make blended whiskies a more fruitful area for experimentation.

Whisky Toddy

A sovereign cure for whatever ails you. At its most simple a whisky toddy can be just whisky and hot water and that is perfect for unblocking noses and troubled sinuses but when served as preventative medicine a little more adventure is called for. In happy coincidence many of the potential ingredients that have medicinal effects also taste delicious in this drink. Lemon juice and zest for vitamin C, honey for its antiseptic and throat soothing qualities and spice to enliven and in the words of eighteenth century quack physicians 'heat the blood'.

50ml blended Scotch whisky
10ml lemon juice
10ml honey
2 dashes aromatic bitters
120ml boiling water or weak tea

Changes in temperature have profound effects on the taste of a spirit or cocktail. Heating ingredients gives every molecule more kinetic energy, more chance to change state from liquid to gas and therefore more opportunity to be experienced as an aroma. It also changes the way we perceive simple tastes. Commercial soft drinks will commonly have six or seven teaspoons of sugar in a serving and are palatable to many. Rarely if ever do you meet someone who would drink a tea or coffee with the same amount of sweetening. This amplification means that care must be taken when making hot drinks. The simplest rule of thumb is to use about half the amount of sweet and sour ingredients that you would use in a cold version; it is also safe to add considerably more water to the mixture than would be included if the recipe was shaken with ice and served cold.

Pour the whisky, lemon and honey into a handled hot drink glass or, if circumstances demand, into your favorite mug. Add the boiled water (or weak tea) and stir. Dash the bitters on the surface of the drink and garnish with a piece of lemon zest studded with three or 4 cloves.

This drink will work with all styles of blended whisky and even with lighter Speyside malts. Due to the dilution and the flavour amplification a robust blend with a good portion of Islay malts makes an intriguing and very palatable version.

Blood and Sand

One of the first examples of a tie-in for a movie, the Blood and Sand was named for the 1922 Rudolph Valentino movie about the life of a bullfighter. It is a rare success when the use of the ingredients in a drink are designed to reference details of an external influence but this drink is one such success. It is also one of the few drinks that uses orange juice, in this case blood orange, to good effect.

Blood orange is still only seasonally available, with the best time to get fresh fruit around Christmas but there are several brands of flash frozen juice available and use of these is suitable in this recipe. If no blood orange is available then regular orange juice can be used but it will need to be soured slightly with the addition of five percent fresh lemon juice. The colour of the drink will not be affected too much as both the cherry liqueur and vermouth will contribute some red notes. The original recipe calls for Cherry Heering, a liqueur made with both the flesh and stones of cherries. If a more vibrant colour is required, and, given the strong character of the Scotch whisky that dominates this drink, try locating a bottle of Luxardo's Sangue Morlacco, a wonderful deep red liqueur made from Marasca cherries.

25ml blended Scotch whisky
25ml cherry liqueur
25ml sweet vermouth
25ml blood orange juice

Shake all ingredients with ice, strain into a chilled cocktail glass, garnish with a cocktail cherry and, for extra theatre, the flamed zest of an orange. This is a simple and effective way to create a wow factor. Cut a small circle of orange peel, leaving an amount of pith to give it structural integrity. Hold the peel ready to be expressed between two fingers and gently heat the peel with a lighter or match. When small jets of flame from exploding sacs of essential oil begin to occur, squeeze the twist sharply expelling all the oils, which will ignite in an impressive fireball. Just remember to use un-waxed fruit for this (and all other garnishes), as wax will burn with an unpleasant aroma.

This recipe works well with a full-bodied blended Scotch whisky, with a fair amount of age. There are several twelve-year-old brands that would be perfect. If you prefer a younger style of whisky try increasing the quantities of the whisky and reducing all the other ingredients by the same amount.

The Penicillin

Created by Sam Ross, the protégé of the late, lamented Sasha Petraske, the Penicillin is certainly the most famous and one of the best modern classic drinks created in the post millennium cocktail revolution. Sasha's bartending was characterized by a thoughtfulness that often led to ingredients being used to their best effect. Sam has carried on these principles and they are very evident in this cocktail. One of the few drinks to call for a strongly peated Scotch whisky, it is used where it matters, to just provide intrigue on the fist sip and as an aromatic tincture. The name of the drink comes from the technique. The drink is 'inoculated' with drops of Islay whisky in the mode of a pharmacist pipetting onto a petri dish, ensuring the ingredient is exactly where it needs to be.

50ml blended Scotch whisky
20ml lemon juice
10ml ginger syrup
10ml honey Syrup
5ml Islay whisky

The ginger syrup is homemade. Use a centrifugal juicer to juice fresh ginger and mix equal parts of the resultant juice by weight with sugar. Shake all but the Islay and strain over ice into a large rocks glass. Carefully drip the Islay whisky onto the surface of the drink and garnish with a piece of candied ginger on a cocktail stick.

When making a Penicillin you are essentially creating a new blended whisky, by adding the Islay. Try using a lighter style of blended whisky, one with plenty of heather honey notes to work with the sour ingredients. The use of ginger does mean that the other ingredients will stand up to a more powerful blend though. The Islay can be from any of the distilleries on the island but Laphroaig works particularly well.

EPILOGUE

If it has been rewarding to discover more about what is in the bottles and the stories that surround so many spirits, to look beyond the marketing that has made spirits fashionable and put the style back into cocktails, join the growing number of taste mentors. Discover the many books now written on spirits, equip yourself with a qualification and gain the confidence to share your passion and knowledge with all who care to listen.

INDEX

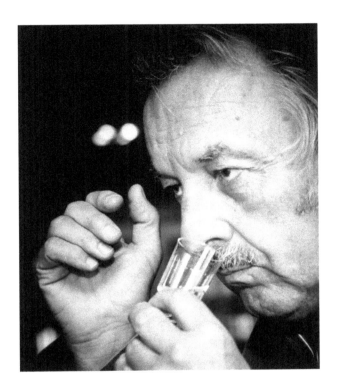

ABOUT THE AUTHOR

During the thirty years he dedicated his life and liver to the corporate world of spirits, Mark worked with many of the world's leading spirit companies including Smirnoff, Hennessy, J&B Rare, Ballantines, Beefeater, Courvoisier, Canadian Club, Bols & Hiram Walker Liqueurs before ending his corporate career by taking Maker's Mark out of America and introducing it around the world, to all who cared to hear about bourbon in general and Kentucky's little gem in particular.

In 1999, Mark left the corporate world and set up Taste and Flavour, a network of renowned speakers, all passionate about spirits and keen to share their knowledge with those wanting to enjoy spirits as potentially memorable drinking experiences and understand better their product realities and histories rather than relying only on brand values to make their choice.

Mark worked with the UK-based global educator, the Wine and Spirit Education Trust, to create the only globally recognized vocational qualification relating to spirits and liqueurs, the Level 2 Certificate in Spirits.

For Mark, spirits, like wines, are to be enjoyed as products of nature rather than the manufacture of marketeers, appreciated as luxuries rather than as alcohol to abuse. To this end he and Taste and Flavour have provided a complement to brand activities, developing brand champions into product authorities, top bartenders into opinion formers, keen amateurs into discerning consumers and empowering all to make the informed choices and recommendations that increase their enjoyment of spirits.

Inspired by this experience, *Spirits Distilled* by Mark Ridgwell and published in 2014 by Infinite Ideas Ltd provides informed and entertaining backgrounds to where and how spirits have moulded social history, how spirits are made and why they differ in taste, where the raw materials generate distinctive character and regions or local practice creates individuality.

Spirits are in vogue but, for Mark, far too many remain cloaked in mystery, with their product realities all but ignored in favour of their brand values. His mission is to encourage more to get to know them better and to value more what must be key to the enjoyment of any drink, whether to sip and savour or to enjoy long – the base spirit.